Critical Guides to French Texts

59 Molière: Les Précieuses ridicules

Critical Guides to French Texts

EDITED BY ROGER LITTLE, WOLFGANG VAN EMDEN, DAVID WILLIAMS

MOLIÈRE

Les Précieuses ridicules

David Shaw

Lecturer in French
University of Leeds

Grant & Cutler Ltd
1986

Library of Congress Cataloging-in-Publication Data

Shaw, David, 1944-
  Molière, Les précieuses ridicules.

  (Critical guides to French texts: 59)
  Bibliography: p.
  1. Molière, 1622-1673. Précieuses ridicules I. Title. II. Title: Précieuses
ridicules. III. Series.
PQ1839.S48 1986   842'.4   86-22962
ISBN 0-7293-0259-8

I.S.B.N. 84-599-1740-1

DEPÓSITO LEGAL: V. 2.254 - 1986

Printed in Spain by
Artes Gráficas Soler, S.A., Valencia
for
GRANT & CUTLER LTD
55-57, GREAT MARLBOROUGH STREET, LONDON W1V 2AY
and
27, SOUTH MAIN STREET, WOLFEBORO, NH 03894-2069, USA

Contents

Preface

The wealth of scholarship relating to *Les Précieuses ridicules* is a token of the fascination the little play has always held. It would be unrealistic to ignore this volume of criticism, much of which is excellent. On the other hand, there is disagreement as to precisely what Molière is trying to do in *Les Précieuses ridicules* and a number of the assumptions commonly made about the work seem to me to be highly dubious. This book therefore sets out to examine the play, together with some of these often contradictory critical theories, in the light of the known facts. To this end I shall look at the circumstances in which the play was created and contemporary reactions to it, as well as the scope of the satire and how it works on stage.

The meticulous historical and linguistic studies by Dupois and Livet are helpful starting points. Grateful — but not necessarily uncritical — use is also made of the works of Adam, Bray, Lancaster, Lanson and Michaut: these are still invaluable for the theatrical and historical background to *Les Précieuses ridicules*, as are Mongrédien's splendid reference works. For a comprehensive analysis of *préciosité* itself, there is Lathuillère's monumental study; and the best recent critical edition of the play is that of Micheline Cuénin. To all these works, and many others, I freely acknowledge my debt. But, if I am obliged to others for some of the facts, the interpretation of these facts is my own.

Italicised numbers in brackets refer to the numbered items in the Bibliography. The line references given for *Les Précieuses ridicules* correspond to the line numbers of the Bordas edition (*9*).

Introduction

Les Précieuses ridicules was first performed on 18 November 1659. At that time Molière was virtually unknown. The idea of becoming a famous author had probably never entered his head. He was simply a struggling actor-manager trying to keep a toe-hold in the precarious world of Parisian theatre. He had been in Paris for just over a year, having obtained the king's permission to establish his company at the Petit-Bourbon theatre, under the protection of the duc d'Orléans, on 24 October 1658.

For some thirteen years before that, they had been just one of many itinerant troupes of actors touring the provinces. During the long years away from Paris, Molière had become the leader of the company, as well as being its principal actor. The pressure on him was therefore already considerable. His was the task of finding material for his colleagues to act, of attracting an audience and of directing rehearsals; not to mention taking the main role in most of the plays they performed.

By the late summer of 1659, however, in spite of all his efforts, it was clear that the company was barely holding its own. The 1659-60 season had begun with a succession of failures. Just to remain in business the troupe needed to take around 200 *livres* per performance: however, between Easter and November 1659, the takings rarely reached this figure and once actually fell to a disastrous 42 *livres*.

The major problem was a lack of material of suitable quality. Established playwrights were unlikely to entrust their works to a company of unproven ability. Paris already had two permanent theatre companies, the prestigious 'Troupe Royale' at the Hôtel de Bourgogne and the actors of the Marais theatre, to whom Corneille had given most of his works. The competition was fierce and was made more so by the relative smallness of the theatre-going population. Even new plays rarely ran for more than thirty consecutive performances. And Molière had no new plays.

In seventeenth-century France, a playwright retained control over his work only before it was published. After publication, a play was deemed to have fallen into the public domain and could be performed by any company. Authors therefore extracted as many performances as possible from their plays before having them printed. Hence Molière's anger, reflected in his preface, when he discovered that Somaize was planning an unauthorised edition of *Les Précieuses ridicules*.

Of the plays staged by Molière's troupe between Easter and November 1659, over half were comedies, an interesting statistic in view of the prestige and popularity of tragedy and tragicomedy at this time. Molière and his colleagues were always considered indifferent performers of serious plays. 'Ce n'est pas un merveilleux acteur', wrote Tallemant des Réaux, 'si ce n'est pour le ridicule' (*38*, II, p.778). The choice of plays shows that they were conscious that their talent lay primarily in the realm of comedy.

But the comedies of the time were, on the whole, not very distinguished. The mid-seventeenth century was the heyday of burlesque comedy. This form of theatre, of which the crippled poet Paul Scarron was the main inspiration, had grown out of the verbal humour of farce. It was characterised by exaggerated flights of linguistic fancy and outrageous literary parody. The general atmosphere was one of relentlessly escapist fantasy. During 1659, Molière staged three of Scarron's plays, without any great success.

Romantic comedies of intrigue were also still common. In these works, the plot supplied the major interest through its endless complications and surprises. Reflecting fashionable Spanish and Italian sources, these plays tended to be brittle and ingenious rather than comic. Well represented in the works of writers such as Boisrobert and Thomas Corneille, they too figure prominently in Molière's 1659 repertoire.

Admittedly, some of the comedies performed in the late 1650s were not without interest. Corneille's *Le Menteur* and Desmarets's *Les Visionnaires* were both highly amusing plays containing glimmers of the character comedy which Molière was later to develop, and both were performed by Molière's troupe in 1659. But they were not new. *Le Menteur* had been written some sixteen years earlier and *Les Visionnaires* was even older, having been first performed in 1637.

Throughout 1659, therefore, Molière had struggled to make do with revivals of plays of varying quality, written, for the most part, by other people. In the realm of tragedy, it was evident that his company was not in the same class as the Hôtel de Bourgogne; and in comedy they had the problem of material which, even when it was of good quality, was inevitably past the first flush of youth. Between Easter and November 1659, Molière staged a total of twenty-two different plays, a worryingly high figure, which reflects the crisis the troupe was facing.

Of all the plays they performed at Paris before *Les Précieuses ridicules*, the most successful were the two literary comedies — *L'Etourdi* and *Le Dépit amoureux* — which Molière had written to swell their repertoire during the provincial years. According to La Grange, these plays provided what success the troupe enjoyed largely because they were new to Parisian audiences.

By the autumn of 1659 it must therefore have been clear that new material was necessary if the company was to do more than survive at Paris. To make maximum use of their talents, the new play should ideally be a comedy. As Molière himself had already written two tolerably successful comedies, it made sense for him to undertake to compose another. And, as he had recently secured the services of the famous farce actor Jodelet, it was logical to include in the new play elements of farce along the lines of the 'petits divertissements' that he was accustomed to devising and producing in the provinces.

These, then, are the external circumstances which, in all probability, led to the creation of *Les Précieuses ridicules*. In 1659, Molière had written little and published nothing. There is no indication that he ever entertained any literary ambition, as such, or that he suddenly took it into his head to reform society by means of a quixotic attack on some of its leading personalities. The decision to write the play seems to have been a highly professional response to a crisis within his company: if someone else had brought him a new play in the autumn of 1659, it is arguable that *Les Précieuses ridicules* would never have been written. His preface makes it clear that he was forced against his will to become a published author: but he was an inventive actor and troupe director literally until his dying day. And it was as actor/director that he devised *Les Précieuses ridicules*. If one accepts this initial premiss, the play itself becomes less of an enigma.

1. Comedy

i) *Sources*

When composing *Les Précieuses ridicules*, Molière seems to have used a highly original combination of sources: literary comedy, fashionable society itself and the farce tradition. Admittedly, his enemies sought to undermine the play's success by accusing him of plagiarism, but it is difficult to take this accusation seriously. It was claimed, for example (*35*, II, p.26), that Molière's work was just a copy of a farce by the abbé de Pure, allegedly staged by the Italian troupe in 1656. But almost nothing is known about this mysterious play and we are entitled to wonder whether it ever existed.

If it really was performed in 1656, it seems to have made little impression: Loret, who was favourably disposed towards the abbé de Pure, does not mention it in his *Muze historique*. It is therefore difficult to assess the truth of the allegation that *Les Précieuses ridicules* was based on it. Somaize, from whom the idea seems to have originated, is not a reliable authority and the play itself is lost. That in itself is interesting: it suggests that, at the very most, the abbé de Pure's play can only have existed as a *canevas*, a rough outline from which the Italian actors improvised their performances. Had it ever existed in written form, one suspects the author would have produced it in 1660 to demonstrate that it had inspired Molière. Instead, the only indication of what the abbé de Pure's play may have contained comes from Somaize. In *Les Véritables Précieuses*, one of his characters insists on the similarity between *Les Précieuses ridicules* and the earlier play:

C'est la même chose, ce sont deux valets tout de même qui se déguisent pour plaire à deux femmes, et que leurs maîtres battent à la fin; il y a seulement cette petite

différence que, dans la première [i.e. in de Pure's play], les
valets le font à l'insu de leurs maîtres, et que dans la
dernière [*Les Précieuses ridicules*], ce sont eux qui le leur
font faire. (*35*, II, p.26)

One might argue that such a 'petite différence' is actually rather
major! The intrigue of Molière's play, such as it is, derives its
coherence from the decision of La Grange and Du Croisy to take
revenge on Cathos and Magdelon for their impertinence.

It is possible that the lost farce by the abbé de Pure is the play
referred to in the latter's novel *La Prétieuse* in which 'une fille se
trouvait préférer un faux poète à un galant effectif' (*30*, II,
p.73). In any event, this brief account is probably all that
Molière could have known of the earlier play: in 1656 he was
absent from Paris and it is not easy to see how else he could have
known about a farce apparently improvised in a foreign
language, which passed virtually unnoticed and which was
neither printed nor written down. In all probability therefore,
the influence of the abbé de Pure on *Les Précieuses ridicules* was
extremely slight.

Two plays, on the other hand, which may well have been in
Molière's mind are Chappuzeau's *Le Cercle des femmes* and
Scarron's *L'Héritier ridicule*. Both contain features which recur
in *Les Précieuses ridicules* and both were extremely well known
to Molière. *Le Cercle des femmes* contains an assembly of blue-
stockings, a snobbish heroine determined to marry a nobleman
and whose father is opposed to her passion for literature, and a
rebuffed suitor who seeks revenge by disguising a peasant as a
nobleman. The play is an important curiosity in that it is a farce
which contains satire. Previous seventeenth-century French
farces had invariably stuck to buffoonery and sought only to
amuse. But *Le Cercle des femmes* satirises affected women and
men who ape a rank to which they have no right. It is not a satire
of contemporary manners but an adaptation for the comic stage
of five dialogues taken from Erasmus's *Colloquia*: the heroine is
therefore learned rather than *précieuse*. On the other hand,
Chappuzeau's play may well have given Molière the idea of
putting in a farce something more than horse-play and sexual

innuendo. It was published in 1656, in Lyons, where Molière was then living. It may even have been written to be performed by Molière and his troupe. In any event, they must have known the play well.

Scarron's *L'Héritier ridicule* is an amusing comedy first performed in 1648 or 1649 and revived by Molière in August 1659, three months before the first performance of *Les Précieuses ridicules*. Like *Le Cercle des femmes*, it contains a rejected lover: the latter dresses up his valet as a rich and vulgar suitor, not for revenge, but to find out whether the heroine loves anything but money. There is also a comic servant, who is scathingly critical of the amazing cosmetics favoured by the 'Dames de prix':

> Blanc, perles, coques d'œuf, lard et pieds de mouton,
> Baume, lait virginal et cent mille autres drogues.
>
> (V,i)

One is reminded of Gorgibus's angry comment in *Les Précieuses ridicules*:

> Je ne vois partout que blancs d'œuf, lait virginal, et mille autres brimborions que je ne connais point. Elles ont usé ... le lard d'une douzaine de cochons ... et quatre valets vivraient tous les jours des pieds de mouton qu'elles emploient. (sc.III, ll.58-62)

Moreover, the acting ability of Filipin, the valet in *L'Héritier ridicule*, is established in the same way as that of Mascarille:

> Je sais, quoique laquais, dire sort et destin,
> Parlet Phœbus, écrire, en vers ainsi qu'en prose,
> Appliquer bien ou mal une Métamorphose.
>
> (II,v)

La Grange, it will be remembered, says of Mascarille:

> C'est un extravagant qui s'est mis dans la tête de vouloir

faire l'homme de condition. Il se pique ordinairement de
galanterie et de vers et dédaigne les autres valets, jusqu'à
les appeler brutaux. (sc.I, ll.34-37)

In the light of these similarities of subject and text, not to
mention that of the titles, it is tempting to conclude that Molière
was thinking of *L'Héritier ridicule* when he composed *Les
Précieuses ridicules*.

Another major source might be described as upper class
society in general and Sorel's *Lois de la galanterie* in particular.
Like the farces of Molière's Italian friends, his play contains
many specific references to contemporary society. The satire is
not restricted to *préciosité*: it is also concerned with
pretentiousness in a wider context. As well as being *précieuses
ridicules*, Cathos and Magdelon are ridiculous social climbers,
while the 'marquis de Mascarille' is primarily a foolish aristo-
crat. Even the latter's title is significant. In 1659, the title of
marquis was completely devalued. According to Scarron, 'c'est
la chose du monde dont je voudrais le moins jurer, en un temps
où chacun se marquise de soi-même' (*32*, p.54). Which explains
why Molière was able to claim that 'le marquis aujourd'hui est le
plaisant de la comédie' (*L'Impromptu de Versailles*, sc.1). By
presenting Mascarille as a ridiculous marquis, he was therefore
in little danger of giving offence to anyone that mattered. And
Magdelon's delight at the prospect of a visit by a marquis ('Ah!
ma chère, un marquis!' (sc.VI, l.195)) is a token of her lack of
sophistication.

Numerous other precise allusions to contemporary society
help to define and focus the various forms of pretentiousness on
display. For example, Mascarille is affecting the manner of the
highest ranking courtiers when he speaks of attending the king's
petit coucher (sc.VII, l.240), the exclusive nightly ceremony to
which only the most privileged were admitted. Magdelon's
reference to a 'madrigal sur la jouissance' (sc.IX, l.320) seems to
be an allusion to a notorious sonnet on this theme written by
Mlle Desjardins: this work had appeared in the *Recueil des
pièces choisies* — to which Magdelon refers in the same scene
(l.300). The battles mentioned by Mascarille and Jodelet were

still recent memories: the siege of Arras (sc.XI, l.576) had taken
place just five years earlier, while that of Gravelines (sc.XI,
l.591) had occurred in August 1658. Magdelon naturally
assumes that Mascarille's ribbons are supplied by the fashionable haberdasher Perdrigeon (sc.IX, l.478), whose fame is
attested by many contemporary writers. Such allusions, in
addition to being amusingly topical in their day, help to create
an impression of authenticity which prevents the flights of fancy
from getting out of hand.

But Molière was evidently not content to settle for topical
allusions. For the character of Mascarille, he seems also to have
made use of Sorel's *Les Lois de la galanterie*: a new edition of
this treatise on upper class manners had appeared in 1658, just a
year before *Les Précieuses ridicules*, and its influence on
Molière's text is clearly felt, sometimes almost word for word.
As soon as Mascarille arrives, for example, he declares that he
fears 'Quelque vol de mon cœur, quelque assassinat de ma
franchise' (sc.IX, l.269), and then:

> *après s'être peigné et avoir ajusté ses canons.* Eh bien!
> Mesdames, que dites-vous de Paris? (sc.IX, ll.284-85)

In *Les Lois de la galanterie* we find an almost identical passage:

> Après que vous serez admis et que vous aurez fait vos
> premiers compliments, il sera bienséant de tirer de votre
> poche un grand peigne de corne, dont les dents soient fort
> éloignées l'une de l'autre, et de peigner doucement vos
> cheveux, soit qu'ils soient naturels ou empruntés.
>
> (*36*, p.82)

A few pages later, Sorel offers advice on how to appear an
arbitor of taste:

> Pour faire l'habile, vous nommerez ordinairement tous les
> savants de Paris, et direz qu'ils sont de votre connaissance
> et qu'ils ne font point d'ouvrage qu'ils ne vous com-
> muniquent pour avoir votre approbation. (p.88)

Which sounds remarkably like Mascarille's boast that 'C'est la coutume ici qu'à nous autres gens de condition, les auteurs viennent lire leurs pièces nouvelles pour nous engager à les trouver belles et leur donner de la réputation' (sc.IX, ll.444-47). And again, as Mascarille offers to 'promener ces Dames hors des portes' (sc.XI, l.601), Sorel recommends the would-be *galant* to know 'en quelle saison l'on va promener à Luxembourg et en quelle autre aux Tuileries; quand commence le cours hors la porte Saint-Antoine et dans les bois de Vincennes' (p.76). I could easily continue these comparisons: *Les Lois de la galanterie* also includes detailed instructions concerning powdered wigs, canons, ribbons and other items of the *petite-oie*, the novelty and convenience of the sedan chair ('dernière et nouvelle commodité si utile' (p.14)) and the need to take the ladies to the theatre.

It is however clear that Molière is not merely copying Sorel. He is applying a process of comic amplification and distortion to basically unexceptional material: Sorel's subtle observations concerning the manners and fashions of the leisured classes are transformed, in Mascarille's mouth, into strident affirmations of vanity and snobbery. For example, Sorel gently suggests that perfect good taste can only be acquired in Paris: '... ce ne sera que dans Paris ... qu'il faudra chercher la source et l'origine de la vraie galanterie et où l'on croira que sont les vrais galants' (p.46). Molière transforms the idea into a famous statement of metropolitan snobbery: 'hors de Paris il n'y a point de salut pour les honnêtes gens' (sc.IX, l.290). The advice on how to acquire perfect manners thus becomes a fatuous claim that, outside the capital, manners do not exist: although based on Sorel, Mascarille's crass generalisation about the 'honnêtes gens' demonstrates that he is not of their number!

Similarly, Sorel's advice to 'faire voir les nouvelles pièces de théâtre aux Dames' (p.81), is developed by Molière into a joyous sideswipe at the conduct of certain aristocrats at the theatre and at the declamatory style of his rivals, the actors of the Hôtel de Bourgogne. Mascarille admires their ability to 'faire ronfler les vers' (sc.IX, l.468) and the way they stop to invite applause at the end of set-piece speeches. This was a fairly audacious ploy

on Molière's part and helps to explain the professional hostility
he encountered at the time of *L'Ecole des femmes*. Mascarille's
claim that Molière's actors are 'des ignorants qui récitent comme
l'on parle' (sc.IX, 1.466) is an amusing reference to the more
naturalistic style of Molière's troupe: by having Mascarille
dismiss the new style with his customary impertinence, Molière
is obviously arguing in its favour. But professional polemic is
not allowed to take over. As with the references to society, as
with the borrowings from Sorel, it is perfectly adapted to the
requirements of the comic situation. It is just the kind of daft
thing that Mascarille *would* say!

The third, and most important, source of *Les Précieuses
ridicules* is the farce tradition. Mlle Desjardins calls it *La farce
des Précieuses* (*14*) and the only source suggested by Molière's
contemporaries was the farce allegedly performed by the Italian
troupe. Grotesque characters ridiculed by the ingenuity of others
were a farce commonplace. The substitution of valet for master
was another familiar device: Scarron's farcical comedy *Jodelet
ou le maître valet*, first performed in 1643, was still in Molière's
repertoire in 1659.

Apart from the basic situation, many other important features
of *Les Précieuses ridicules* were obviously borrowed from the
world of farce. A one-act play in prose, it was written to be performed after a longer work. The characters bear the names of
the actors who created the roles and at least one of them
originally wore a mask. Beatings abound and, if we are to
believe Mlle Desjardins, some of the humour in the early performances was robust to the point of crudity. All these features
were to be found either in the farces which Molière had recently
performed at Lyons or in those of the Italian troupe, with whom
he had shared the Petit-Bourbon theatre until July 1659. We
shall be considering the relationship between *Les Précieuses
ridicules* and the farce tradition in the following section.

The sources of *Les Précieuses ridicules* were therefore extra-
ordinarily varied, involving literary comedy[1] as well as farce,

---

[1] In addition to the plays by Chappuzeau and Scarron, Lancaster mentions
possible borrowings from Tristan, Thomas Corneille, Brosse, Guérin de Bouscal
and Quinault (*21*, III, p.219).

carefully documented aspects of the manners of the leisured classes as well as their language. Such a combination was breathtakingly original: its success was to have a tremendous bearing on Molière's subsequent career.

ii) *Mask*

Three of the characters in *Les Précieuses ridicules* needed little introduction to contemporary playgoers: Mascarille, Jodelet and Gorgibus were already familiar figures on the Parisian stage. They were associated with the individual actors who created them: in the case of Jodelet, Julien Bedeau had been tirelessly playing the character for over twenty years. In this respect, they are related to the stock types, or *masks*[2], of Italian farce. Throughout the first half of the century, Parisian farce had been dominated by the Italian tradition, known as the *commedia dell'arte*. Italian troupes frequently visited Paris, where they were greatly appreciated for their inventive slapstick and for the expressiveness of their *masks*. In the preface to *Les Précieuses ridicules*, Molière's almost casual reference to three of these stock types — the Doctor, the Captain and Trivelin — demonstrates how famous they were. Of all the *masks* of Italian farce, the valets were by far the most popular.

By the 1630s, the great French farce actors at the Hôtel de Bourgogne also had their *masks* and, like the Italians, were known by the name of the single character they had created. Robert Guérin, for example, achieved national fame as Gros-Guillaume, the drunken, naive, good-humoured valet he always played; and Henri Legrand was equally celebrated as Turlupin, also a valet but a witty, roguish one. The dominance of the valet type was a clear sign of Italian influence. Turlupin actually wore a mask, in the Italian manner, whereas Gros-Guillaume preserved the white-face tradition of the sixteenth-century French farce.

This tradition was continued, after Gros-Guillaume's death, by Jodelet, another *enfariné*. This remarkable actor created yet

---

[2] To avoid ambiguity, I shall use *mask* thus to refer to the stock types of Italian farce; mask thus will have its normal meaning of face covering.

another valet *mask*, that of a vulgar, boastful coward. The latter became so famous, with his white face, black moustache, nasal whine and increasingly emaciated appearance, that leading playwrights, such as Scarron and Thomas Corneille, wrote plays around him: for many years, his name in the title of a new play[3] more or less guaranteed its success. He alone kept farce alive in the capital when it went out of fashion around the middle of the century. Molière was probably delighted to acquire his services, at Easter 1659, as Jodelet was the one comic actor whose presence in a rival troupe he had cause to fear. He was by now an old man, having begun his career over fifty years before; and, as he was to die early the following year he may well have been in poor health. This would explain the brevity of his role in *Les Précieuses ridicules*.

However, when the 'vicomte de Jodelet' was announced, a seventeenth-century spectator would have known precisely what sort of character to expect. The aristocratic title would have seemed a splendid contradiction in relation to a character known for his vulgarity and cowardice: Jodelet's name had not been previously mentioned but, as his *mask* was essentially that of a valet, the audience would have realised that, like Mascarille, he was not a true nobleman. This element of complicity between the *mask* and the spectator is underlined by the outrageous pun on 'gens de service' (sc.XI, l.569), which Cathos and Magdelon naturally fail to notice. There is even a reference in the text to Jodelet's celebrated white face. Mascarille's comment about 'une maladie qui lui a rendu le visage pâle comme vous le voyez' (sc.XI, l.548) is both a good example of the self-conscious humour of farce and a joke at the expense of Cathos and Magdelon, the only people in the theatre not to recognise the loutish valet.

The joke is compounded in the following line, when Jodelet alleges that his illness was the result 'des veilles de la Cour et des fatigues de la guerre'. The coarseness of the Jodelet *mask* was the antithesis of courtly elegance; and his legendary cowardice

---

[3] See, for example, Scarron's *Jodelet ou le maître valet* and *Jodelet souffleté*, d'Ouville's *Jodelet astrologue*, Thomas Corneille's *Jodelet prince* and Brécourt's *Feinte mort de Jodelet*.

meant that the nearest he ever got to battle was boasting about it. All his talk of warfare in sc.XI is therefore an ironic reminder of this famous aspect of his character. It is also implicit in the text when, for example, he scorns the idea of having captured merely a demilune bastion at the siege of Arras and claims to have captured 'une lune toute entière' (l.578): the enormity of the gaffe clearly suggests that his familiarity with warfare is slight.

The coarseness of the character is also evident in the marvellous buffoonery, reminiscent of Italian *lazzi*, in which he is involved. The contest he initiates with Mascarille to see who can show the most impressive scar culminates in the latter threatening to remove his breeches. And, when the two valets are unmasked and stripped at the end of the play, Jodelet is found to be wearing about a dozen shirts, the last of which is traditionally that of a cook. When reduced to this, he puts on a cook's hat, which he has been carrying in his belt, and kneels respectfully before Cathos, who pushes him away in disgust. In one version of this highly amusing piece of 'business', which might well go back to the seventeenth century, the half-naked Jodelet, shivering with cold, then attempts to warm his hands on the footlights.

The tone of the play therefore becomes appreciably more earthy as soon as Jodelet appears. Unlike Mascarille, he is incapable of using *précieux* language: the nearest he gets to it is his crude pun about bleeding from his 'veine poétique' (sc.XI, l.630). His joke about meeting Mascarille when the latter was a cavalry commander on a galley is the more amusing if one sees it as a reference to past misdemeanours: the only galleys Jodelet and Mascarille would know are those reserved for convicts. When he mentions alleged feats of arms, he discusses them in the crude manner of a simple soldier. He delights in talking about his wounds, in getting Cathos to feel his leg and in revealing increasing amounts of his scrawny anatomy. His vulgarity is even worse than that of the prosaic Gorgibus, but the girls are too naive to notice. On the contrary, entirely won over by Mascarille's outrageous charade, they see in Jodelet's visit another sign that they are becoming fashionable: 'Ma toute bonne, nous commençons d'être connues: voilà le beau monde qui prend le chemin de nous venir voir' (sc.XI, ll.532-34). The Jodelet *mask* is thus used to demonstrate, with particular brutality, the unreality of the girls' pretentions.

Unlike Jodelet, Gorgibus is a *mask* type who seems only to have featured in plays by Molière: before *Les Précieuses ridicules*, the character had appeared in *La Jalousie du Barbouillé* and *Le Médecin volant* and he would also feature in *Sganarelle* and in the lost farce *Gorgibus dans le sac*. The Gorgibus role seems to have been played by Jodelet's brother L'Espy: he is always a stolid old-fashioned guardian figure seeking in vain to impose his authority and reacting with anger or incomprehension to the madness going on around him. A tightfisted, homespun merchant at heart, the character is faintly reminiscent of the *Pantalone* of Italian farce.

In *Les Précieuses ridicules* he is thus predictably scandalised at the amount of money being squandered on cosmetics (sc.III). His prosaic materialism is the antithesis of the girls' pretentiousness. His *mask* therefore helps the first comic sparks to fly. The romantic fantasies of Cathos and Magdelon appear the more ludicrous in the presence of this obtuse and self-centred provincial who mortifies them by insisting they marry as soon as possible and by mistaking 'le bel air' for a musical term (sc.IV, l.84); and the vanity of their jargon is neatly highlighted by its juxtaposition to Gorgibus's earthy language, rich in vigorous terms like 'concubinage', 'graisser le museau' and 'balivernes'. His blanket condemnation of 'romans, vers, chansons, sonnets et sonnettes' as 'pernicieux amusements des esprits oisifs' (sc.XVII, l.745) is as grotesque as the girls' own infatuation with them. Far from signifying Molière's opinion, this is part of the Gorgibus *mask*. His namesake in *Sganarelle* says precisely the same thing:

De quolibets d'amour votre tête est remplie;
Et vous parlez de Dieu bien moins que de Clélie.
Jetez-moi dans le feu tous ces méchants écrits,
Qui gâtent tous les jours tant de jeunes esprits.

(ll.29-32)

Both Jodelet and Gorgibus are thus skilfully used to point the satire. Although amusing in themselves, they are not allowed simply to 'do their turn' but serve, through effects of juxtaposition and contrast, to define the folly of the two girls. On the other hand, their roles are clearly limited by the conventions of their *masks*. They are essentially figures of farce, fixed types without subtlety or depth. Although well-integrated into the action of the play, they are not characters in the deeper sense of the word.

Mascarille is clearly different. The first memorable character in Molière's theatre, he was a major reason for the success of *Les Précieuses ridicules*: the play was even occasionally referred to as *Le Marquis de Mascarille*. The role represents a crucial development in Molière's career. Like Jodelet and Gorgibus, however, Mascarille is basically a *mask*. The character had already featured prominently in both *L'Etourdi* and *Le Dépit amoureux* as a resourceful, witty valet reminiscent of Turlupin. *L'Etourdi* is actually little more than a succession of ingenious schemes dreamed up by Mascarille to further his eponymous master's ill-fated love-affair. The capable valet, full of vitality and roguish self-confidence, even devises a Latin inscription to celebrate his own talents: 'Vivat Mascarillus, fourbum imperator!' (l.794). This motto is equally apt to describe the final, and most interesting, incarnation of Mascarille, in *Les Précieuses ridicules*.

The Italian ancestry of the character is implicit in his very name. The Italian word *maschera* can mean either mask or *mask* and its diminutive form *mascherina* means a small mask. And Molière does actually seem to have worn a mask to play the part. The Dutch astronomer Christian Huyghens made this note in his diary after attending a performance of *Les Précieuses ridicules* on 28 January 1661: 'A la comédie au Palais-Royal, vu jouer *Sancho Pansa* ... Et *Les Précieuses ridicules* de Molière. Mascarille masqué, le [vi]comte enfariné' (*27*, I, p.141). Huyghens's terse note establishes an interesting fact: over a year after the first performance of *Les Précieuses ridicules*, the spectators were still being treated to a confrontation between a masked character and a white-face in the manner of the

Italianate farces at the Hôtel de Bourgogne thirty years before. Molière had restored a grand old tradition which the public evidently loved.

But Mascarille is far from being just a nostalgic tribute to the farces Molière had seen in his youth. Before *Les Précieuses ridicules*, the *mask* convention embraced costume: Arlequin always wore clothes covered in a colourful triangular check pattern and Gros-Guillaume was never seen without his red cap, white blouse and striped trousers. But Mascarille has no set costume. In *Les Précieuses ridicules* everything about his appearance is designed to suggest a parody of the dress worn by court fops. The costume is therefore part of the satire rather than a feature of the *mask*. This kind of systematic visual parody was unheard of in a French farce; hence the surprised tone of Mlle Desjardins's description:

> ... sa perruque était si grande, qu'elle balayait la place à chaque fois qu'il faisait la révérance, et son chapeau si petit, qu'il était aisé de juger que le marquis le portait bien plus souvent dans la main que sur la tête; son rabat se pouvait appeler un honnête peignoir, et ses canons semblaient n'être faits que pour servir de caches aux enfants qui jouent à cline-musette; et en vérité, Madame, je ne crois pas que les tentes des jeunes Massagètes [in *Cyrus*] soient plus spacieuses que ses honorables canons. Un brandon de galants [i.e., a cluster of ribbons] lui sortait de sa poche comme d'une corne d'abondance, et ses souliers étaient si couverts de rubans qu'il ne m'est pas possible de vous dire s'ils étaient de roussi [Russian leather], de vache d'Angleterre ou de maroquin; du moins sais-je qu'ils avaient un demi-pied de haut, et que j'étais fort en peine de savoir comment des talons si hauts et si délicats pouvaient porter le corps du marquis, ses rubans, ses canons et sa poudre. (*14*, p.129)

Not a trace therefore of the servant costume worn in *L'Etourdi*. As with the linguistic satire, the visual parody consists of a grotesque amplification of authentic upper-class fashion. Mlle

Desjardins's description of Mascarille's costume features many of the elements (canons, wig, plumes, ribbons and large jabot) missing, according to Cathos, from those of La Grange and Du Croisy. These items really did represent the very latest fashion. Wigs, for example, were still a novelty in 1659: Louis XIV only began to wear one in 1673. Molière simply exaggerates these trends to the point of absurdity.

This tension between tradition and originality is also a feature of Mascarille's character. Like his namesake in *L'Etourdi*, he shows astounding inventiveness and self-confidence. But, whereas his predecessor had dazzled by the sheer number and variety of the schemes he dreamed up, the Mascarille of *Les Précieuses ridicules* is delightful for the wholehearted way he enters into a single piece of deception. The fop he portrays has much in common with the 'real' foolish aristocrats that we meet in other plays by Molière. Like Acaste, in *Le Misanthrope*, the 'marquis de Mascarille' is vain, snobbish, impertinent, obsessed with his appearance, despises those who study and draws attention to himself at the theatre. He uses fashionable language, writes mediocre verse, like Oronte, and complains about his valets, in the manner of Alceste. This is obviously the more amusing for our knowledge that Mascarille is really a valet himself; but it is quite in keeping with the role he is playing.

However, to what extent he is actually aware he is playing a role is left interestingly uncertain. We know from La Grange that he is 'un extravagant qui s'est mis dans la tête de vouloir faire l'homme de condition' (sc.I, l.34). Mascarille himself is therefore presented as an eccentric, with ideas above his station. According to his master, 'il dédaigne les autres valets, jusqu'à les appeler brutaux' (l.36), which suggest he may not be consciously playing a part when he refers to the porters as 'marauds', 'faquins' and 'canailles' (sc.VII). It is as if the fact of dressing and being treated as a nobleman is sufficient finally to persuade him that he is worthy of that rank. When he prides himself on his elegance, literary talent and influence, he is all the funnier because he seems actually to believe what he is saying. The final unmasking therefore marks the end of his dream as well as that of Cathos and Magdelon.

On the other hand, we can never completely forget that he is really just a servant in disguise. He slaps the porter and seeks to avoid payment, as a gentleman might: but he pays up as soon as he is himself threatened with violence, very much the reaction of a valet. His impromptu is memorably dreadful, far more incompetent than Oronte's sonnet in *Le Misanthrope*: and his grotesque analysis serves only to emphasise the poem's inadequacy. Inventive though his conversation is, his fund of compliments and anecdotes is evidently limited: when Jodelet is announced, he is already beginning to repeat himself. His 'Quoi! toutes deux contre mon cœur en même temps!' at the end of sc.IX (ll.506-15) is essentially a repetition of the 'Quelque vol de mon cœur' routine at the beginning of the scene (ll.269-75).

He often inadvertently reminds us of his origins by his choice of language. This process can be very subtle. In Mascarille's first scene, for example, the porter refuses the challenge of an imperfect subjunctive: '... vous avez voulu aussi que nous soyons entrés jusqu'ici' (sc.VII, ll.211-12). This construction, however, holds no such horrors for Mascarille: 'Voudriez-vous, faquins, que j'exposasse l'embonpoint de mes plumes aux inclémences de la saison pluvieuse, et que j'allasse imprimer mes souliers en boue?' (sc.VII, ll.213-16). The imperfect subjunctive was undoubtedly favoured by the upper classes in seventeenth-century France. But to put two such ugly examples in the same sentence is obviously going too far: it shows a fundamental ignorance of the niceties of polite usage. Mascarille is trying too hard.

He also gives himself away by more obvious linguistic lapses, which jar splendidly with the generally pretentious tone of the conversation. 'Pic, repic et capot' (sc.IX, l.256), for example, is an expression drawn from piquet, a card game particularly favoured by the lower classes: it contrasts well with 'tout ce qu'il y a de galant' in the same sentence. After the entry of the unsophisticated Jodelet, Mascarille's language becomes even more uneven: 'nos libertés auront peine à sortir d'ici les braies nettes' (sc.XI, l.619) provides a marvellous clash between *précieux* abstraction ('libertés') and barrack-room humour ('les braies nettes' [with clean breeches], a joke which refers to the colic-inducing effects on young soldiers of coming under fire).

The curious duality of the character is not wholly resolved at the end of the play: even when unmasked and beaten, Mascarille never actually reverts to being merely a valet. On the contrary, he now strikes the grandiloquent pose of a great man unjustly wronged: 'O Fortune! quelle est ton inconstance!' (sc.XV, l.705). The contrast between the pomposity of the sentiment and the humiliation of the unmasking is obviously very funny; but the stylised simplicity of 'fourbum imperator' has been left far behind. Mascarille's final speech begins 'Traiter ainsi un marquis!', and he exits protesting that vain appearance is preferred to 'la vertu toute nue' (sc.XVI, l.736). As he is an impostor, and now a half-naked one at that, the joke is a good one. But his amusing façade of injured dignity remains more or less intact, and we are left wondering whether this gifted clown will ever go back to being a simple valet.

The *mask* has therefore become almost invisible. It no longer dominates the role but simply provides a source of comic tension. The Mascarille in *L'Etourdi* is just a comic type, a valet demonstrating how clever he is; the Mascarille of *Les Précieuses ridicules*, on the other hand, is much more a true comic character making a brilliantly sustained attempt to pass himself off as something he ultimately can never be. He has stretched the *mask* to breaking point.

Molière was to acknowledge this in two ways. On the one hand, he ceased to play the role masked. Whereas Chauveau's frontispiece to the 1666 edition shows Mascarille wearing a mask, that of the 1682 edition shows him, still recognisable in wig and costume, but with Molière's face, unmasked. In addition, there would be no more Mascarille characters. The *mask* of the cunning valet obviously permitted a wider range of comic situations than those of Jodelet or Gorgibus: but, for all his brilliance, Mascarille can only *imitate* members of other social classes, he can never *be* them. His range is still limited. Molière therefore abandoned this particular *mask* and adopted another, that of Sganarelle, a much more flexible type, sometimes valet, sometimes woodcutter, sometimes foolish old man, who was to appear in no fewer than six of his plays. He in turn would be abandoned, after *Le Médecin malgré lui* in 1666, as the successive Sganarelle characters were becoming increasingly idiosyncratic. They had transcended the *mask* convention.

This tendency is already implicit in the Mascarille of *Les Précieuses ridicules*. On the one hand, as so frequently happened with the more illustrious *masks*, Molière came briefly to be known by the name of his creation. On the other, Mascarille marks the beginning of the transition in Molière's theatre from farce types to comic characters. Perhaps, therefore, François Doneau was not so wide of the mark when, writing in 1660 after all, he declared Mascarille to be 'une des choses la plus ingénieuse [sic] qui ait jamais paru au théâtre' (*27*, I, p.132).

iii) *Comic structure*

It might be argued that the idea of the *mask* pervades the whole of *Les Précieuses ridicules*: like Mascarille, Jodelet and Gorgibus, the other characters also have names which reflect the identity of the original actors. For that reason, as we shall see, the names Cathos and Magdelon have no more satirical significance than those of La Grange and Du Croisy. Even Marotte conforms to this pattern: the name is a diminutive form of Marie and the role was created by La Grange's future wife, Marie Ragueneau. In most of these cases, the identification of player with character seems to have gone slightly beyond the matter of their names.

For example, the slightly curious basic structure of three contrasting pairs of characters reflects Molière's need to give appropriate roles to all his leading performers. This seems to have been a real problem at the start of his Parisian career, particularly in respect of the rivalry between his three principal actresses. Writing to Molière in the spring of 1659, Chapelle speaks of:

> le déplaisir que vous donnent les partialités de vos trois grandes actrices pour la distribution de vos rôles. Il faut, tâchant de faire réussir l'application de vos rôles à leur caractère, remédier à ce démêlé qui vous donne tant de peine. (*27*, I, p.110)

In November 1659, Marquise Du Parc having moved to the
Marais theatre, the troupe was reduced to just two leading
ladies, Madeleine Béjart and Catherine de Brie. In addition, the
troupe had recently acquired the services of La Grange and Du
Croisy, two actors of considerable talent. If we add the two
principal clowns, Molière himself and the legendary Jodelet, the
troupe's major talents clearly tended to fall into three pairs. This
is no doubt why Molière doubled the number of main parts that
he found in the plays by Chappuzeau and Scarron.

Within each pair of characters, there is a degree of contrast.
The roles of La Grange and Du Croisy are just sketches,
designed to give the play a framework and to justify the
appearance of Mascarille in disguise. But, of the two, La Grange
is clearly the dominant partner. He does virtually all the talking
in the opening scene and it is he who organises the revenge. He
also initiates the beating and stripping of the valets at the end of
the play. The authority and articulacy of La Grange the
character may well reflect the easy manner of La Grange the
actor. The latter's instinctive grace and cultured speech were
such that he took most of the 'romantic lead' parts in Molière's
troupe. He succeeded Molière as orator in 1664 and, three years
later, was the actor chosen to plead for the banned *Tartuffe*
before the king. The shortness of his role in *Les Précieuses
ridicules* reflects the fact that the romantic interest is here
reduced almost to nothing in favour of satirical comedy.

The roles of Cathos and Magdelon are more evenly matched.
Their reactions and comments are amusingly similar. Their
obsession with an artificial code of behaviour is neatly underlined by the way they echo each other's sentiments: they share
the same background and their knowledge of polite society is
entirely second-hand, gleaned from the same romantic novels.
The speech of both is rich in grotesquely used examples of
upper-class language, interspersed with half-understood
scientific terminology, such as 'chromatique' (sc.IX, 1.421),
wrongly given a feminine gender, and with the odd hint of
lower-class usage, such as Magdelon's 'cela n'est pas de refus'
(sc.IX, 1.441).

On the other hand, there are perceptible differences between them. Their tastes in novels are slightly different: Magdelon seems to favour *Cyrus*, while Cathos alone mentions *Clélie*. Cathos is the less independent of the two, endlessly reinforcing or agreeing with what her cousin has just said. Her speeches therefore tend to begin with formulae such as 'En effet, mon oncle', 'Il est vrai, mon oncle', 'Assurément, ma chère', 'Et pour moi, quand je me regarde aussi', etc. When Magdelon comments that Mascarille 'est le caractère enjoué', Cathos simply embroiders the idea with a pedantic reference to a character in *Clélie*: 'Je vois bien que c'est un Amilcar' (sc.IX, l.277). And, whereas Magdelon expresses petulant anger during the final revelations, Cathos remains almost completely silent.

In addition, while Magdelon dreams of a world of ritualised, platonic purity, Cathos is distinctly more aware of physical reality. If Magdelon describes at length the esoteric conventions of *précieux* love, Cathos is more concerned about how their suitors are dressed. She also thinks of providing seats for their guests and is prepared to use a workaday term like 'miroir' to communicate with the servant. Even if she recoils from the idea, she has at least had the thought of sleeping 'contre un homme vraiment nu' (sc.IV, l.165), she admits, to Magdelon's evident embarrassment, 'un furieux tendre pour les hommes d'épée' (sc.XI, l.572) and is prepared to touch Jodelet's enormous scar (sc.XI, l.583).

This hint of a suppressed interest in the physical world provides a pleasant contrast with her cousin's more consistently abstract romanticism. As we shall see, one of the criticisms levelled at the *précieuses* was that of hypocrisy. This contrast would have been highlighted, in 1659, by the relative youth of Catherine de Brie — at 29, she was 12 years younger than Madeleine Béjart — and by her undisputed beauty. Nevertheless, Magdelon's role is the funnier of the two. Her speeches are slightly longer than those of her cousin, she invariably speaks first and seems generally the more eccentric. She describes in grotesque detail (sc.IV, ll.91-121) her ideal world of romantic, carefully choreographed love-affairs, dreams of discovering that she is of noble birth (sc.V, l.181) and talks incessantly of 'le beau monde', to which she is desperate to belong. However, for all the talk of literature, she is not really concerned with culture or taste as such: 'je ne donnerais pas un clou de tout l'esprit qu'on peut avoir' (sc.IX, l.327). Her only interest in frequenting witty people is because 'ce sont eux qui donnent le branle à la réputation' (sc.IX, l.310). She wants to know about the latest literary works only because 'C'est là ce qui vous fait valoir dans les compagnies' (sc.IX, l.326). The vulgarity of the social climber is more clearly defined in Magdelon than in Cathos. In addition, although Magdelon does not pepper her speech with *précieux* adverbs in the same way as Cathos, she does tend to use sillier, more memorably funny terms than her less strident cousin. Expressions such as 'le conseiller des grâces' (sc.VI, l.202) and 'les commodités de la conversation' (sc.IX, l.264) are ludicrous enough in themselves: addressed to a servant, they underline the extent to which she has lost touch with reality.

The role is one of the funniest female parts in Molière's theatre. Second only to Mascarille in comic impact, the part of Magdelon is in fact longer than his. A comic female role of this importance was most unusual on the Parisian stage before 1659. In the old farces, comic hags and servants were usually played by men in disguise: the actor Alizon had specialised in this kind of role. But, in Madeleine Béjart, Molière had a vastly experienced colleague who was reputedly the best actress in the country. Now aged 41, she was growing a little old for romantic parts and would increasingly apply her talent to important comic roles, such as Dorine and Cléanthis. She was in effect the first French comic actress of note and it was her unusual versatility which made the character of Magdelon possible.

The greatest contrast of all is that between Mascarille and Jodelet. In 1659, Molière was 37 and at the height of his acting powers: Julien Bedeau was around 70 and possibly ailing. Mascarille therefore dominates the play while Jodelet's role is subdued. When they are together, in sc.XI, it is the brilliant Mascarille who controls the flow of the conversation, while Jodelet appears very much his subordinate. He simply returns the compliment when Mascarille mentions his bravery. When Mascarille suggests a country excursion, he merely agrees. Asked his opinion of Magdelon's eyes, he simply defers to

Mascarille: 'Mais toi-même, marquis, que t'en semble?' (sc.XI, 1.618). And it is probably significant that, when Mascarille arrogantly asserts that the violinists are 'violons de village', Jodelet meekly complains that they are playing too fast for him because 'je ne fais que sortir de maladie' (sc.XII, 1.664).

The relationship between the characters in *Les Précieuses ridicules* and the original actors is therefore a close one. The casting of even the minor roles seems to have been a potential source of comedy. Thus, when Jodelet enters, Magdelon calls to Almanzor for 'le surcroît d'un fauteuil': 'Allons, petit garçon, faut-il toujours vous répéter les choses?' (sc.XI, 1.544). This is a pretentious reference to the contemporary fashion for employing young boys as lackeys: the line would have been the funnier, in 1659, for the fact that Almanzor was originally played by the actor De Brie, a burly 52 year-old. Many aspects of the play were therefore conditioned by the actors available to Molière. This was obviously a consistent feature of his plays: every part he created was conceived with a particular player in mind. But few of his works bear the mark of this tendency as clearly as *Les Précieuses ridicules*.

With these three pairs of characters, Molière created a play which is both simple and beautifully constructed. The central confrontation is obviously that between the two girls and the two valets. We have here two pairs of phonies in opposition: would-be *précieuses* entertaining bogus noblemen. This permits a wider range of comic possibilities than if either pair had been the genuine article. Real *précieuses* prided themselves on their ability to assess the merit of others: quite apart from the pretentiousness of their own language and sentiments, the biggest gaffe committed by Cathos and Magdelon is therefore that they remain unaware of their guests' essential vulgarity. 'Que tout ce qu'il dit est naturel!' says Magdelon (sc.XI, 1.622), after one of Mascarille's more convoluted compliments.

The action takes place 'dans cette salle basse' (sc.VI, 1.199), that is, in a downstairs room. Real *précieuses* received their guests in a specially appointed first-floor room, complete with day-bed, *ruelle* and *alcôve*. Cathos and Magdelon appear the more ridiculous for having no such room at their disposal. The detail also offered the practical advantage of avoiding the need for a change of scene.

Our curiosity is aroused by the talk of revenge in the opening scene. We thus hear of the girls' bizarre manner before we meet them and we gather that the trick will involve the 'extravagant' Mascarille. But La Grange is interrupted before he can explain his plan and we are left wondering what he has in mind. Then follow three contrasting scenes, linked by the uncomprehending Marotte, which underline different aspects of the girls' silliness by juxtaposing them in turn to the three *mask* characters. The scene with Gorgibus points the contrast between their prosaic origins and their bookish fantasies. Their contempt for Gorgibus, confirming La Grange's description, means they merit the punishment which begins in the long scene with Mascarille. Although the brilliant valet constantly gives himself away, the girls are entranced by his rank, his promises, his manner, his language and his appearance. Their gullibility fuels his self-confidence and he reaches new heights of mock-genteel absurdity with the analysis of his impromptu and his simpering pride in his appearance. Jodelet is kept in reserve to bring the play to a climax: if Mascarille's vulgarity is strongly hinted at, that of Jodelet is unmistakable. But still the girls suspect nothing. They are entranced by the prospect of acceptance by polite society and their excitement reaches its height with the improvised ball. They are then brought back to reality, in the starkest possible manner, with the arrival of their former suitors and the beatings that ensue. The end quickly follows, after a flurry of highly visual activity.

However, if the tempo certainly increases during the final scenes, the visual quality of the whole play is very striking. The three *mask* characters look consistently bizarre: Mascarille in mask and extravagant costume, Jodelet with his white face and Gorgibus dressed in old-fashioned clothes. Mascarille is constantly on the move, flourishing his comb, adjusting his canons, leaning to left and right as he listens to the girls, offering his hands for them to savour his perfumed gloves and bending low for them to appreciate his wig. Several pieces of comic business were doubtless developed into full scale *lazzi*: Mascarille's

impromptu, his dancing display, Mascarille and Jodelet
undressing to show their scars and the pantomime surrounding
Jodelet's shirts all offer great scope to inventive actors. All the
entrances are memorably rumbustious: Gorgibus constantly in a
noisy rage, Mascarille greeting Jodelet with protracted
histrionics, the armed intervention in the midst of the music and
dancing and, best of all, Mascarille crashing through the door in
his sedan chair. The mock violence of farce constantly breaks
through the spurious gentility of the setting. Mascarille's role
begins and ends violently. He slaps the porter, he and Jodelet are
beaten up by their masters and then Gorgibus beats the
violinists. *Les Précieuses ridicules* is therefore an intensely visual
play. It is essentially a finely crafted farce, full of vitality and yet
refreshingly simple, despite the variety of sources from which it
borrows. But in two respects, the work takes farce into completely new territory. In Mascarille, as we have seen, we have a
brilliant creation who stretches the principle of *mask* to the
threshold of character comedy. And the fact that so much of the
comedy has its origin in social satire is in itself sufficient to set
Les Précieuses ridicules apart from the French farces which
preceded it. Let us now consider this aspect of the play in more
detail.

2. Satire

i) *Préciosité*

If one of the sources of *Les Précieuses ridicules* was seventeenth-century polite society in general, it is clear that the play is specifically concerned with the phenomenon known as *préciosité*. What exactly was this and what is the nature of Molière's comment on it? In his preface, he claims that his play contains only 'satire honnête et permise' (l.44): how do we reconcile this with the frequently stated view that *Les Précieuses ridicules* contains attacks on identifiable individuals?

The *précieuses* were actually prominent for less than a decade, following the resumption of salon society after the Fronde. Before the civil war, French polite society had been dominated by the splendid salon of Mme de Rambouillet, famous for the brilliant conversation of its members. After the war, however, it was no longer the force it had been and, throughout the 1650s, the most influential salon was that of the famous novelist Madeleine de Scudéry. Her *Samedis* were less aristocratic, less instinctively tasteful than the elegant gatherings at the hôtel de Rambouillet. Mlle de Scudéry herself was known as Sapho, after her self-portrait in *Cyrus*, and all her friends adopted pseudonyms, such as Théodamas and Philoxène, in a systematic, rather pedantic manner that would not have been tolerated by Mme de Rambouillet. There is undeniably a reminiscence of this ponderous trend in the pseudonyms adopted by Cathos and Magdelon.

Romantic literature, just one form of entertainment among many at the hôtel de Rambouillet, was the main concern of Mlle de Scudéry's salon. The *cercle mondain* had given way to the *cercle littéraire*. The meetings invariably included a reading, by Sapho herself, of the latest passage of *Cyrus* or *Clélie*, just as Mascarille recites his impromptu. Many of the conversations in the novels actually took place in the salon. These tended to revolve around esoteric questions of love psychology: for example, the famous *Carte de Tendre*, referred to by Cathos in sc.IV of *Les Précieuses ridicules*, grew out of the tortuous courtship that Mlle de Scudéry imposed on the hapless Pellisson. It must sometimes have been hard to tell where the literary salon ended and romantic literature began.

Mlle de Scudéry's *Samedis* therefore come closest to the image of the *précieux* salon reflected in *Les Précieuses ridicules*. But they also mark the culmination of a tendency established at the hôtel de Rambouillet and distorted by the unpleasantness of the civil war. All the salons, whether presided over by the aristocratic Mme de Rambouillet, the intellectual Mlle de Scudéry or one of her many imitators, were frequented by a self-confessed élite. Around the middle of the century, they tended to be concerned only with delicacy of thought and expression, were separated from ordinary people by an increasingly purified language, took no interest in the real problems of society and remained intent on the enjoyment of their artificial world of refinement and sensibility. In these circumstances, it was inevitable that some members of the salons should take the principle of refinement too far.

However, very few women of the time can be positively identified as *précieuses*. As the word generally had pejorative overtones, no-one ever admitted belonging to this category. One critic has estimated the number of true *précieuses* to be as low as seven (*16*, p.23)! The most frequent use of the word was as a term of abuse designed to belittle members of the rival group or salon. For example, the word is not to be found anywhere on the *Carte de Tendre* but is very much in evidence in the numerous parodies to which the work gave rise. In Bussy-Rabutin's *Carte du pays de Braquerie*, the Précieuse is a river separating the land of the Braques from that of Prudomagne: that is, it lies between prudery and madness! Such parodies tended to emanate either from the racy circle of Gaston d'Orléans or from the abbé d'Aubignac's group of crusty misogynists, to whom Mlle de Scudéry's idealised portrayal of love psychology was quite intolerable. Similarly, when Mlle de Montpensier condemns the *précieuses*, she is thinking of Mlle d'Aumale and Mme de Fiesque, whom she detested and, for Bussy-Rabutin, the *précieuses* are his enemies Mlle de Guise, Mme de Montausier and Mme d'Olonne. In these circumstances, the objective meaning of the word is extremely difficult to define.

ii) *Literary type*

We are on safer ground if we concentrate on the meaning given to the word by seventeenth-century writers. The three characteristics of the *précieuses* most frequently commented on by their contemporaries are affected speech and manners and prudery, all of which feature in *Les Précieuses ridicules*. The type is first mentioned in a letter written by the chevalier de Sévigné, dated 3 April 1654: 'Il y a une nature de filles et de femmes à Paris que l'on nomme Précieuses, qui ont un jargon et des mines, avec un déhanchement merveilleux' (*34*, p.246). Such references to the jargon of the *précieuses* are fairly common: according to the princesse de Montpensier, for example, 'Elles ont quasi une langue particulière' (*28*, p.304). However, precise examples of the language they used are more difficult to find. The few expressions mentioned by reliable authorities tend to be variants on just three or four types of hyperbole: adjectives and adverbs indicating an extreme degree of feeling ('adorable', 'insupportable', 'furieusement', 'terriblement', etc.), rhetorical questions conveying acuteness of sensibility ('on n'en meurt pas?', 'le moyen de ...?'), adjectives used as abstract nouns and often reinforced by a favourite superlative ('le tendre', 'le dernier doux') and effusive greetings, such as the ubiquitous 'ma chère'; to which one might add a taste for using verbs of action to convey abstract ideas ('donner dans un raisonnement', 'parer l'esprit', etc.).

From the scant evidence available, it therefore seems that the *précieuses* favoured a kind of hyperbolical vagueness designed to demonstrate their rejection of commonplace sentiments. But, as we shall see, there is no evidence that anyone spoke exactly like Cathos and Magdelon.

References to the affected manner of the *précieuses* are also common. Sévigné speaks of their 'déhanchement merveilleux' and Maulévrier, in his *Carte du Royaume des Précieuses*, names Façonnerie as the kingdom's capital. The princesse de Montpensier speaks of their 'affectation déplaisante' and claims that 'elles penchent la tête sur l'épaule, font des mines des yeux et de la bouche' (*28*, p.303).

But the favourite target for satirical remarks was the hostility of the *précieuses* towards physical love. A character in La Fontaine's comedy *Clymène* complains she has to pretend to be in love 'pour éviter le nom de précieuse ... cette qualité odieuse' (*19*, p.38). And Faure accuses Mlle de Rambouillet, with her friend Mlle d'Aumale, of waging war on love:

> Précieuses, vos maximes
> Tyrannisent nos désirs.
> Rambouillet, et vous Daumale,
> Quoi ne verrons-nous jamais
> L'Amour et votre cabale
> Faire un bon traité de paix?

(*15*, p.57)

Unlike the *prude*, however, the *précieuses* did not reject all forms of love. They were quite happy to enter into platonic relationships and sought to portray themselves as experts in these mysterious domains. Scarron calls them 'ces Jansénistes d'amour' (*31*, I, p.237), and Saint-Evremond, waspishly linking their romantic prudery to a suggestion of hypocrisy, claims that their real achievement, 'c'est à aimer tendrement leurs amants sans jouissance, et à jouir solidement de leurs maris avec aversion' (*8*, p.78).

The picture that emerges from contemporary references to *précieuses* is therefore one of mannered prudes endlessly fascinated by the subtleties of platonic love and speaking in hyperbolic abstractions. However, we have seen how difficult it is to distinguish between living reality and polemical myth. If the *Samedis de Sapho* seem to resemble most closely the stereotype of a *précieux* salon, it is important that we do not simply take d'Aubignac's word for it.

It is but a short step from this kind of confusion to the creation of a literary type, a simplified, stylised image of an elusive social reality. Faure is already moving in this direction when he talks of the '*cabale* des précieuses', which makes it sound as if the *précieuses* had formed a coherent group or sect: there is no evidence to support this.

Equally disconcertingly, several authors distinguish between true and false *précieuses*. In his *Epître chagrine au Maréchal d'Albret*, Scarron says:

> Mais revenons aux fâcheux et aux fâcheuses,
> Au rang de qui je mets les précieuses,
> Fausses s'entend, et de qui tout le bon
> Est seulement un langage ou un jargon.
>
> (ll.131-34)

And Molière himself gave nine performances, in 1660, of a play by Gilbert entitled *La Vraie et la Fausse Précieuse*, which has not survived. This unexplained, and apparently artificial, distinction was probably a literary precaution designed to avoid giving offence to powerful real *précieuses*. In *Les Précieuses ridicules*, Molière does essentially the same thing: he justifies the distinction implicit in the title by emphasising the provincial origins of his heroines.

This process of stylisation is especially evident in the abbé de Pure's novel *La Prétieuse*. The work is a long and immensely subtle satire of *préciosité*, which draws together most contemporary attitudes on the subject. The irony is so gentle as to be sometimes almost imperceptible and some critics have actually argued that the novel is really a tribute to the *précieuses*. However, even in the most overtly complimentary passages, one is aware of a slight over-effusiveness, which betrays the author's true intentions. As, for example, when he repeatedly stresses the newness of the term *précieuse*: 'C'est un mot du temps, un mot à la mode' (*30*, I, p.12). Elsewhere, the satire is more obvious. The *précieuses* are shown relentlessly seeking 'des bons mots et des expressions extraordinaires' (I, p.71), passing solemn judgement on various shades of sentimentality (I, p.353), placing labels on smiles (II, p.162) and railing unrealistically against the 'slavery' of marriage (I, p.281). Paternal authority over women is stridently reviled (II, p.268, etc.) and all the characters have pompous pseudonyms based on Greek words (I, p.375). Mlle de Scudéry is fulsomely described as 'la Muse de notre siècle et le prodige de notre sexe' (I, p.143) and the suggestion that women should live in a state of total promiscuity (II, p.23) sounds suspiciously like a parody of the hostility towards marriage expressed in *Cyrus*.

The germ of *Les Précieuses ridicules* is therefore already contained within the pages of *La Prétieuse*. De Pure's novel even contains two references to the possibility of satirising the *précieuses* in play form. One of his characters says: 'Nous n'avons qu'à ériger notre compagnie, assembler notre troupe, et nous mettre en état de contrecarrer ces Précieuses, de tourner en burlesque leurs conversations, faire même comédie de leurs personnes, de leurs actions et de leurs discours' (I, p.354). Later on, Aurélie, who is clearly a *précieuse ridicule*, is taken to the theatre and is mortified to find that the subject of the comedy is her own behaviour: the Italian actors perform the play, called *La Précieuse*, in which '... une fille se trouvait préférer un faux poète à un galant effectif et de condition, et qui par une erreur d'esprit donnait au mérite de ses ouvrages et de ses notions, ce qu'elle ôtait au droit des gens du siècle qui suivent les sens et l'apparence' (II, p.173). This sounds remarkably like the 'plot' of *Les Précieuses ridicules*: the possibility that Molière took the basic idea for his play from this very sentence cannot be totally discounted. In any event, *La Prétieuse*, of which the final part was published in 1658, demonstrates that the *précieuse* was established as a literary, and specifically comic, type at precisely the time when Molière was beginning to look around for a subject.

iii) *Focus*

In spite of the existence of the *précieuse* as a literary type, most critics have ignored Molière's claim that *Les Précieuses ridicules* contains only 'satire honnête et permise'. It has been repeatedly asserted that the play is a personal attack against identifiable members of the salons, and the favourite candidates are Mme de Rambouillet, Mlle de Rambouillet and Mlle de Scudéry.

The case against Mme de Rambouillet apparently rests entirely on her name, Catherine de Vivonne: it has been suggested that the name Cathos signifies a personal allusion (*6*, p.16). There is, however, no contemporary evidence to support this interpretation. Cathos, like all the other characters in the play, takes her name from that of the person who first played the part: in her case it was Catherine de Brie.

In addition, we know that the hôtel de Rambouillet was well represented at the first performance of *Les Précieuses ridicules*: the group may well have included Mme de Rambouillet herself. This would surely not have been the case had there been any possibility of Mme de Rambouillet being publicly humiliated. A few years later, on 16 March 1664, she summoned Molière and his troupe to perform two plays at her house, a further indication that *Les Précieuses ridicules* had not been seen as an attack on her. In any case, by 1659, her salon had long ceased to dominate polite society. She was still universally loved and respected, but hers was no longer the name on everyone's lips. It is therefore difficult to see why Molière, newly arrived in Paris, should have wished to ridicule her.

It is equally unlikely that the play was seen as an attack on Mlle de Rambouillet. The case for such a hypothesis rests largely on Tallemant's comment that she was 'un des originaux des *Précieuses*' (*38*, II, p.894). We also know from Tallemant that she was a dreadful snob, with an offhand manner towards guests: '... elle est maligne et n'a garde d'être civile comme sa sœur' (I, p.473). These two remarks are sufficient for Antoine Adam, in a famous essay, to conclude that Molière must have had her in mind: 'L'accueil impoli que les Précieuses infligent à deux honnêtes gens devait viser directement Angélique-Clarisse d'Angennes [Mlle de Rambouillet], qui avait ce défaut de mal recevoir les gens' (*10*, p.45). This seems to me a totally unjustified assumption. It has been convincingly argued (*8*, p.21) that Tallemant's reference to something called *Les*

Précieuses was probably written *before* the first performance of *Les Précieuses ridicules*. In addition, Tallemant twice mentions a *historiette* he intended to write on the subject of the *précieuses*:

> ... je prétens finir par Madame la Princesse, Madame de Longueville et les Précieuses.
> Nous parlerons d'elle [de Mlle de Rambouillet] dans *l'Historiette* de Voiture et dans celle des Précieuses. (*38*, I, pp.584 and 473)

Mlle de Rambouillet was evidently going to figure prominently in this essay, which in fact never appeared. It is therefore likely that Tallemant's remark about her being 'un des originaux des *Précieuses*' refers, not to Molière's play, but to his own unpublished *historiette*. There is thus no obvious reason to identify the haughty, aristocratic Mlle de Rambouillet with Molière's naive, provincial heroines.

The case for *Les Précieuses ridicules* being a satirical attack on Madeleine de Scudéry is superficially much stronger. Some critics seem to have taken it as a self-evident truth, without really looking at the facts: 'Le nom de Cathos a tout l'air d'avoir quelque signification, mais celui de Magdelon en a certainement une, elle est directe et Madeleine de Scudéry s'y fût difficilement méprise' (*13*, II, p.11). This is not good criticism. As we have seen, the names of all the characters in *Les Précieuses ridicules* reflect the identity of the actors originally playing the roles. La Grange and Du Croisy, for example, were the stage names of the actors concerned. Magdelon was played by Madeleine Béjart. In itself, therefore, the name is no more a reference to Mlle de Scudéry than Cathos is an allusion to Mme de Rambouillet.

Antoine Adam is on equally shaky ground when he concludes that Molière is throwing his weight behind d'Aubignac: '*Les Précieuses ridicules* se rattachent donc à la polémique engagée contre les précieuses par la coterie aubignacienne. C'est directement contre Sapho, contre les habitués du *Samedi*, contre le salon ami de Mme du Plessis-Guénégaud' (*10*, p.44). The latter was undoubtedly on excellent terms with Mlle de Scudéry: the fact that Molière was summoned to perform *Les Précieuses ridicules* before Mme du Plessis-Guénégaud on 4 February 1660 therefore suggests that the latter did not see the play as an attack on either of them. Adam bases his hypothesis on the fact that d'Aubignac speaks warmly of Molière in his *Quatrième Dissertation*: but this work was written in 1663, over three years after the first performance of *Les Précieuses ridicules* and does not mention Mlle de Scudéry. As there is no indication that Molière had any kind of contact with d'Aubignac in 1659, there is thus not a shred of evidence to link *Les Précieuses ridicules* with d'Aubignac's campaign against Mlle de Scudéry.

Equally, critics have sometimes exaggerated the number of allusions to Mlle de Scudéry in the text of *Les Précieuses ridicules*. According to Michaut, for example, when Mascarille proclaims that 'Les gens de qualité savent tout sans avoir jamais rien appris' (sc.IX, l.411) Molière is ridiculing a similar remark in Mlle de Scudéry's self-portrait in *Cyrus*: 'Sans que l'on ait jamais oui dire que Sapho ait rien appris, elle sait pourtant cent choses' (quoted by Michaut, *26*, p.46). This is a very misleading quotation: by putting a capital letter on 'sans', Michaut has made the above passage sound like a complete sentence, whereas it really forms just the second half of a longer and crucially different idea: 'Elle a une telle disposition à apprendre facilement tout ce qu'elle veut savoir que, sans que l'on ait presque jamais oui dire que Sapho ait rien appris, elle sait pourtant toutes choses' (*33*, X, p.333). On the very next page it is emphasised that Sapho's apparently effortless culture is actually the result of good organisation and prolonged study: and she is repeatedly critical of women who delight in ignorance. The wise Sapho thus clearly has nothing in common with Mascarille's fatuous remark about 'gens de qualité'. The latter is simply the kind of joke that Molière was frequently to make about the empty-headed *petits-maîtres*. The foppish Acaste, in *Le Misanthrope*, is equally proud of his ability to 'juger sans étude' (l.792).

Michaut also argues (*26*, p.46) that Magdelon's claim to be 'furieusement pour les portraits' (sc.IX, l.345) is a reference to Mlle de Scudéry, as she launched that particular fashion. Again, the link seems to me unproven. Certainly, by including in her novels thinly-disguised portraits of well-known contemporaries, Mlle de Scudéry probably was responsible for the initial form of the vogue in the early 1650s. But, because of the very popularity of the portrait, she had long ceased to be its only exponent by the time of *Les Précieuses ridicules*. It has been demonstrated (*24*, p.137) that, from about 1657, the name most commonly associated with the portrait was probably that of Mlle de Montpensier, one of the most outspoken critics of the *précieuses*!

It is anyway difficult to see why Michaut feels that Molière is satirising the portrait more than the other minor forms mentioned in scene IX. There are also references to madrigals, sonnets, impromptus and enigmas: the leading exponent of the latter form was Cotin, whose dislike of Mlle de Scudéry was legendary. All these forms were practised and enjoyed in most of the salons, not just in the *Samedis*.

In any case, it is the attitude expressed towards these forms that is being satirised, rather than the forms themselves. Cathos and Magdelon are not ridiculous for being interested in portraits and madrigals. They are, in a sense, ridiculous for *not* being interested in them. They see them less as a source of pleasure in themselves than as a means of gaining a toe-hold in salon society. According to Magdelon, they are simply what one needs to be able to talk about in order to acquire any sort of reputation: 'C'est là ce qui vous fait valoir dans les compagnies et, si l'on ignore ces choses, je ne donnerais pas un clou de tout l'esprit qu'on peut avoir' (sc.IX, ll.326-28). It is the vulgar pretentiousness of Cathos and Magdelon that is being satirised: their attitude towards these literary forms is simply a token of this. Another form mentioned is after all comedy (sc.IX, l.459) and we can probably assume that Molière was not trying to ridicule that form of entertainment!

It seems to me that we should interpret in the same light the references to Mlle de Scudéry's novels. These are quite specific: Magdelon and Cathos intend to be wooed (sc.IV, ll.92-121) in the manner of the protracted courtship ritual described in *Cyrus* and *Clélie*; they judge their suitors by reference to towns on the *Carte de Tendre* (sc.IV, ll.126-28); unlike Marotte, they have

studied 'la filofie dans le grand *Cyre*' (sc.VI, l.191); and
Mascarille is gushingly compared to Amilcar (sc.IX, l.277), one
of the most congenial characters in *Clélie*. But the works of
other novelists are also recalled. Polixène, the name adopted by
Magdelon, is also the main character in a novel by Molière
d'Essertines, published in 1627; Aminte, the name favoured by
Cathos, and Almanzor, the name given to the lacky, are both
names of characters in Gomberville's *Polexandre*, which was
published in 1637.

For the satire is surely aimed, not at a particular author, but at
the two girls who take this escapist fiction so seriously. They
have confused reality and fantasy. Romantic novels are their
only point of reference. They are horrified when the ignorant
Marotte lumps together Latin, philosophy and 'le grand *Cyre*',
blithely confusing the novel *Le Grand Cyrus* with the title 'Sire'.
But this is really just a grotesque reflection of their own attitude.
For them, the only knowledge and philosophy worth considering
is to be found in romantic novels. Marotte has picked up the
idea from them. In the depths of their province, they have come
to assume that these works really do reflect the reality of
Parisian polite society. Having neither the cultural maturity nor
the wit to be themselves, they can only ape the lives of characters
in books.

In this respect, *Les Précieuses ridicules* belongs to a satirical
tradition appreciably older than *préciosité*. The success of
L'Astrée, and the spate of idealistic romances which followed,
inspired a succession of works which poked fun at the artificiality of the convention. After Sorel's *Francion* and *Le Berger
extravagant*, written in the 1620s, the theme was illustrated by
Chappuzeau, in his *Cercle des femmes*, by Desmarets de Saint-
Sorlin, in *Les Visionnaires*, by Furetière, in his *Roman
bourgeois* and by Boileau, in his *Dialogue des Héros de Roman*.
Molière himself would return to the theme in *Les Femmes
savantes*. *Les Précieuses ridicules* is less a personal attack on the
author of *Clélie* than Molière's first attempt to exploit this
traditional theme.

Michaut claims that Mlle de Scudéry was offended by *Les
Précieuses ridicules* (*26*, p.46). But he produces no material to

support this statement and the available evidence seems to suggest exactly the opposite. Molière's troupe was frequently invited to perform before Sapho's friends and protectors. Somaize, who greatly admired Mlle de Scudéry and rarely missed a chance to vilify Molière, says nothing about a personal attack of any kind. And Mlle de Scudéry herself expresses nothing but admiration for Molière. Writing, in the 1680s, about 'l'agréable comédie des *Fâcheux*', she wishes Molière were still alive, to mock as effectively the foibles of the new age (*24*, p.121). In addition, Molière's comedy ballet *Mélicerte* (1666) is based on an episode in *Cyrus*. There is therefore no sign of any animosity between the two writers.

Moreover, *Les Précieuses ridicules* actually espouses a number of the ideals expressed in *Cyrus*. Sapho repeatedly mocks those who use 'des mots barbares' (*33*, X, p.389), her civilised manner is the subject of grotesque imitations (*33*, X, p.350), the ridiculous pedant Damophile sounds very like Magdelon (*33*, X, p.351), and the provincial Amestris, unlike Cathos and Magdelon, is fully aware of the gaffes likely to be committed by the unwary newcomer to polite society (*33*, I, pp.412-13). Far from ridiculing Mlle de Scudéry, Molière's play expresses an attitude which, if we allow for the process of theatrical simplification, bears a striking resemblance to her own. It cannot therefore be seriously argued that *Les Précieuses ridicules* attacks recognisable members of Parisian polite society. On the contrary, Molière takes care to establish in the opening lines that his heroines are pretentious 'pecques provinciales' (sc.I, l.10), newly arrived in the capital and seeking to imitate aspects of upper class manners of which they have little first-hand knowledge. His *précieuses* represent a brilliant development of the literary type mentioned above rather than personal satire. We must therefore concede that he is telling the truth when he claims that the play contains only 'satire honnête et permise'. It is unlikely that he would seek to impress anyone with a pious disclaimer in his preface if the play itself contained hurtful references to real people. There is no solid evidence that contemporaries thought it did.

iv) *Language*

If it is not possible to identify personal satire in *Les Précieuses ridicules*, what of the language spoken by the main characters? It is clear that much of the play's comic appeal lies in the quality of this famous jargon. What makes it work so well? And how does it relate to what we know of the language of the real *précieuses*? One critic has declared it to be authentic: 'Rien de plus vrai, malgré le grossissement nécessaire au théâtre, que le langage de Cathos et de Magdelon' (*23*, p.130). It is difficult to see how he could be so sure: Livet's exhaustive study of the published works and correspondence of the period suggests that *Les Précieuses ridicules* is the sole source of this jargon: 'Nous n'avons plus, après *Les Précieuses ridicules*, aucune preuve que le langage qui leur est prêté par Molière ait été parlé' (*4*, p.41). If this language really had been spoken by such a self-consciously literate section of society, one would have expected to find some trace of it outside *Les Précieuses ridicules*. The idea that it did exist but that, with this one exception, it sank without trace, seems to me unacceptable: the jargon of the *précieuses*, as spoken by Cathos and Magdelon, was almost certainly invented by Molière.

On the other hand, there is no question of this jargon being completely artificial. If that were the case, it would not be so delightfully accessible. Unlike some of the imitations that followed, the language used by Molière's *précieuses* does not require foot-notes: the vast majority of the expressions used by Cathos and Magdelon are to be found in the works of contemporary authors who could not remotely be considered *précieux*. Molière himself uses most of them in other plays without satirical intent.

For example, the military expression 'donner dans' (as in 'donner dans le piège', etc.) found favour with the *précieuses* as a striking way of indicating entry into some kind of sentiment or experience: but it was by no means restricted to them. Thus, if Cathos says, '... ma cousine donne dans le vrai de la chose' (sc.IV, l.124), we also find La Grange saying: '... ils n'auront pas l'avantage de se servir de nos habits pour vous donner dans la vue' (sc.XV, 1.695).

The expression was simply fashionable: it occurs frequently in Molière's plays in situations where it is clearly not meant to seem ridiculous: 'Pour gagner les hommes, il n'est point de meilleure voie ... que de donner dans leurs maximes' (*L'Avare*, I,i); 'Mon Dieu! Prince, je ne donne point dans tous ces galimatias où donnent la plupart des femmes' (*Les Amants magnifiques*, I,ii). In none of these cases is the expression 'donner dans' meant to seem comic: it is simply part of the language of upper-class society.

The same comment applies to 'furieusement', probably the term most frequently associated with the *précieuses*: 'C'est comme le *furieusesment* et le *terriblement* qu'on a employés partout en ces derniers siècles. Les personnes de bon jugement ont bien su se garder de telles fautes' (*37*, p.312). It is therefore no surprise to find that Magdelon is 'furieusement pour les portraits' (sc.IX, 1.345).

On the other hand, we also find Racine saying, in a letter dated 5 September 1660, 'Je crains furieusement le chagrin où vous met votre maladie'. And the term is also used by Scarron, one of the most redoutable critics of *préciosité*: 'L'honneur d'être admis à notre petite société commence à être grand, et à s'échauffer furieusement dans la Cour et dans la Ville' (*25*, II, p.439). While Molière himself often gives the term to characters who are anything but *précieux*: 'Vous m'avez fait faire des souliers qui me blessent furieusement' (*Le Bourgeois Gentilhomme*, II,v); 'Vous donnez furieusement dans le marquis' (*L'Avare*, I,iv). In itself, therefore, the term was clearly not ridiculous.

Another expression frequently associated with the *précieuses* is 'dernier', used to signify 'extreme(ly)'. Cathos and Magdelon certainly favour the term: as Gorgibus's sentiments are described as 'du dernier bourgeois' (sc.IV, 1.80) so Mascarille's madrigals are 'du dernier beau' (sc.IX, 1.357). But, as in the other cases mentioned, this usage was not the exclusive property of people who could be called *précieux*. Livet notes numerous examples of its use in the works of such sober citizens as Pascal, Boileau and Bossuet (*25*, II, p.57). And Molière frequently gives

it to characters, such as Elvire, Alceste and Elise, who are mani-
festly not meant to sound affected.

I could extend this type of demonstration almost indefinitely:
the terms used by Cathos and Magdelon are simply fashionable
expressions belonging to the language of polite society in general
rather than to the *précieuses* in particular.

What then is the secret of the amusing language spoken by the
characters in *Les Précieuses ridicules*? How can it be that it
neither corresponds exactly to the type of speech favoured by
real *précieuses*, nor yet departs from the kind of expressions that
seem to have formed the stuff of elegant social intercourse?

The key would seem to lie in Molière's technique of accumulation. There does not appear to have been a jargon used
exclusively by the *précieuses*, but the latter do seem to have
become excessively fond of a small number of terms already in
polite usage. Expressions like 'furieusement' and 'effroyablement' were particularly favoured because they seemed to express
the extreme sensitivity and general absence of mediocrity with
which the *précieuses* sought to associate themselves.

It is this tendency, suitably amplified, which makes the
language of Cathos and Magdelon so funny: the terms they use,
unremarkable in themselves, are abused and repeated to the
point of absurdity. 'Furieux' and 'furieusement' are thus used
relentlessly, not to mention variants such as 'tout à fait',
'terriblement', 'diablement', 'comme un démon', 'effroyable',
'effroyablement' and 'le plus agréablement du monde'. The
overall effect is one of incongruously sustained hyperbole which
serves only to underline the pretentiousness of the speaker.

In addition to the comic effect of simple repetition, these
expressions are often the more amusing because of the inappropriate contexts in which they are used. Cathos's description of
Mascarille's plumes as 'effroyablement belles' (sc.IX, l.494) is a
splendid contradiction in terms, as are Magdelon's 'délicatesse
furieuse' (sc.IX, l.499) and Cathos's 'furieux tendre' (sc.XI,
l.572). In these examples, the language is being both devalued,
by the use of 'effroyablement' etc. to describe something
relatively insignificant, and pulled in two directions at once by
the ludicrous association of terms.

But many of the most amusing lines in *Les Précieuses ridicules* derive their impact from an effect of accumulation, a heaping-up of fashionable terms to produce a concentration which is clearly ridiculous. When, for example, Molière uses the term 'donner dans' in other plays, it is invariably followed, as we have seen, by a simple noun expressing a tangible concept, such as 'maximes' or 'galimatias': it thus passes virtually unnoticed. Cathos and Magdelon, on the other hand, tend to use it in association with substantified adjectives and abstract nouns: 'ma cousine donne dans le vrai de la chose' (sc.IV, l.124); 'nous n'avons garde ... de donner de notre sérieux dans le doux de votre flatterie' (sc.IX, ll.259-60). The contrast between the triviality of the sentiments and the vulgar pretentiousness of the language used is magnificent. While none of these terms are particularly amusing in themselves, the effect of such an accumulation is hilarious.

Time and again, Cathos and Magdelon — and, for that matter, Mascarille — demonstrate their real lack of breeding by jumbling together fasionable terms in ludicrous combinations. 'Pousser les beaux sentiments', for example, was one of the very first vogue expressions to be associated with the *précieuses*. As early as 1652, Scarron speaks mockingly of:

> ... une sorte de gens fâcheux qui se sont depuis peu élevés dans Paris, et qui se font appeler *pousseurs de beaux sentiments*. On ne demande plus si on est honnête homme, on demande si on pousse les beaux sentiments.
> (*25*, III, p.341)

Another favourite expression was 'débiter', in the sense of 'speak eloquently'. One of the abbé de Pure's heroines says, of a *précieux* gathering, 'on y forme de belles notions, et la manière de les débiter' (*30*, I, p.10). And we have noted that the *précieuses* tended to favour abstract nouns based on adjectives. Magdelon gives a splendid demonstration both of her desire to appear refined and of her lack of true refinement by combining *all* these features of *précieux* speech in one sentence: 'il faut qu'un amant... sache débiter les beaux sentiments, pousser le doux, le tendre et le passionné' (sc.IV, ll.94-96). The terms themselves are unexceptionable, if slightly hackneyed: it is through the wanton piling-up of clichés that Magdelon gives herself away.

The same can be said even of the most outrageous line in the play: 'voiturez-nous ici les commodités de la conversation' (sc.IX, l.264). In her desire to avoid an expression as banal as 'apporter', Magdelon can only find 'voiturer', which usually meant to transport (people) in a carriage. To tell a servant to do it to a chair is obviously ludicrous. Moreover, a 'chaise de commodité' was a particular kind of armchair. Magdelon omits the concrete term 'chaise' and adds the more abstract word 'conversation'. The effectiveness of the sentence stems from the juxtaposition of two such pieces of affectation, which creates an impression of concentrated silliness. On the other hand, for all the pretentiousness of the jargon, Molière has skilfully avoided obscurity. The way the words are used is sufficient to make Magdelon sound ridiculous but not enough for the sentence to become incomprehensible.

This combination of comedy, clarity and authenticity is achieved in a slightly different way when Magdelon refers to a mirror as 'le conseiller des grâces' (sc.VI, l.202). The term was already in existence but was normally used in conjunction with 'miroir'. Thus:

> Amarille, en se regardant
> Pour se conseiller de sa grâce
> Met aujourd'hui des feux dans cette glace
> Et d'un cristal commun fait un miroir ardent.
>
> (*25*, I, p.463)

As with 'commodités de la conversation', Magdelon omits the concrete term ('miroir') and adds an unremarkable verb used in an affected way: 'venez nous tendre ici dedans le conseiller des grâces'. The servant girl naturally finds the order incomprehensible: 'Par ma foi! je ne sais point quelle bête c'est là' (l.203). Molière thus derives maximum comic effect from the most esoteric expression of all by placing it next to Marotte's plebeian bluntness. He also prudently manages to explain the meaning of the jargon and, at the same time, underline its artificiality, by having Cathos contemptuously translate it into everyday French, ostensibly for Marotte's benefit: 'Apportez-nous le miroir, ignorante que vous êtes' (l.205).

Molière's jargon is therefore neither invention nor copy. Although no-one ever spoke exactly like Cathos and Magdelon, their language is recognisable as reflecting *précieux* usage. The latter seems to have consisted of the frequent use of just a few fashionable expressions. Molière has seized upon this tendency and amplified it: through a skilful process of accumulation and juxtaposition, he pokes fun at its pretentiousness without lapsing into obscurity.

The very fact that he chose to spotlight *précieux* jargon is probably significant. Before *Les Précieuses ridicules*, the characteristic of the *précieuses* most frequently commented upon was their rejection of physical love. This is certainly hinted at in Molière's play: Cathos, for example, is shocked by the very idea of sleeping 'contre un homme vraiment nu' (sc.IV, l.164). But neither she nor Magdelon is totally opposed to marriage in the way, for example, that Armande will be in *Les Femmes savantes*. Molière has singled out the less prominent, and less controversial, feature of language: which supports the thesis that he was not concerned with personal satire. All members of polite society could appreciate the witty parody of certain linguistic trends; but as no-one really spoke like Cathos and Magdelon, no-one was likely to take the joke as a personal attack.

The impact made by Molière's parody of *précieux* language is demonstrated by the success of Somaize's *Les Véritables Précieuses*, which is basically just an unsubtle exploitation of this feature of *Les Précieuses ridicules*. The quality of the linguistic humour in Molière's play betokens a conscious effort to raise the 'petit divertissement' above the unsophisticated level of entertainment with which it had previously been associated. The idea of combining social satire and verbal humour with the techniques of farce was astoundingly original. It was to prove rather more successful than Molière had anticipated.

3. Towards Publication

i) *Performance*

It was the success of *Les Précieuses ridicules* that forced Molière to begin to publish his works. And the play's unusual early career suggests that this success took him by surprise. It was first staged in the spacious Petit-Bourbon theatre on Tuesday 18 November 1659, after a performance of Pierre Corneille's *Cinna*. This was the first time that Molière had offered two plays to the Parisian public in a single session, although he had frequently done this in the provinces. For the spectators in the Petit-Bourbon, the double bill must therefore have seemed something new and original. Thirty years earlier, tragedies at the Hôtel de Bourgogne had regularly been followed by the bawdy farces of Gros-Guillaume, Gaultier-Garguille and Turlupin. But, by 1659, Parisian farce was virtually dead, killed off by the official moral austerity of the time, of which *préciosité* was one manifestation. As far as Parisian spectators were concerned, *Les Précieuses ridicules*, obviously too short a play for Molière ever to have considered playing it by itself, was therefore a bold experiment.

On the other hand, the muted circumstances in which the work was first performed suggest that Molière did not anticipate the impact it would make. For one thing, he chose to launch it on a Tuesday, the quietest of the three *jours ordinaires*, the normal performance days in seventeenth-century Paris. The theatres tended to present new plays on a Friday in order to whet the public appetite and thereby ensure a good attendance on the following Sunday. Of the fifty-three new plays staged in Molière's theatres, thirty-nine had their première on a Friday. But *Les Précieuses ridicules* was evidently not considered worthy of this treatment. In addition, Molière omitted to raise prices for the first performance. For new plays, it was quite normal to double the prices, both of seats and of standing room in the *parterre*. Although he seems to have observed this custom with his other plays, Molière again apparently thought *Les Précieuses ridicules* too modest an offering to deserve such an honour.

Even at normal prices, however, the new play with its intriguing title swelled the takings to 533 *livres*, still a modest sum but over a third more than they had ever taken before. A week earlier, when *Cinna* had been performed by itself, it had brought in just 300 *livres*. But, in spite of this promising start, *Les Précieuses ridicules* was withdrawn after a single performance. It was replaced by a new play, *Oreste et Pylade* by Coqueteau de la Clairière, which was so coolly received that it had to be withdrawn after only three performances.

Les Précieuses ridicules was therefore brought back, on 2 December, in harness with an old play, *Alcyonée*, by Du Ryer. This time Molière did double the prices and the takings leapt to the splendid figure of 1,400 *livres*: they remained high for four more performances. But again, the play was withdrawn to make way for a new tragedy. For the first performance of Magnon's *Zénobie*, the takings plummetted once more and the play's mediocrity was such that, like *Oreste et Pylade*, it lasted just three performances. Molière eventually brought back *Les Précieuses ridicules*, on 26 December, teaming it first with *Zénobie* — a considerable act of generosity towards Magnon — and then with a succession of other plays.

This time the little comedy's success was both incontestable and durable: it was given forty-four performances up to 11 October 1660, when the Petit-Bourbon was closed for demolition, and a total of fifty-three performances on the public stage in less than two years, a marvellous figure for the time. In spite of the absence of the Court, away in the south for the signing of the Paix des Pyrénées, Molière was soon being invited to give performances of *Les Précieuses ridicules* in the houses of the gentry; after his return to the capital, the king saw the play three times in as many months during the summer of 1660 and, on the third occasion, was moved to give the company a gift of 3000 *livres*. The play was as popular at Court as in the public playhouse.

A slight mystery remains, however, concerning the two short interruptions during the play's initial run at the Petit-Bourbon. Why should Molière have chosen to stage two mediocre tragedies in preference to a play which was evidently more successful with the public than anything he had presented before? One of his enemies hinted darkly that it was banned (*35*, I, p.189), but there is no indication that this claim was anything but a piece of mischief. The interruptions were almost certainly the result of a feature of French theatre which *Les Précieuses ridicules* would begin to undermine, the automatic prejudice in favour of tragedy. A new tragedy was theoretically bound to provoke sufficient interest for the appendage of a 'petit divertissement' to be unnecessary. Tragedy was still considered the noblest form of theatre and a tragic author, conscious of his prestige, would scarcely have been pleased to find his play associated with a mere farce; especially if, as seems likely, *Les Précieuses ridicules* originally contained some rather crude jokes which did not find their way into print. Molière himself was doubtless keen to refute the idea, gleefully proclaimed by his rivals, that he was just another *farceur*. He was still essentially an actor and, in 1659, it must have seemed as if a successful acting career could only be built upon serious plays. He therefore doubtless preferred to keep *Les Précieuses ridicules* in reserve, rather than risk offending those rare authors prepared to trust him with their tragedies. It thus took him over a month to accept that he had himself written the successful play his company needed.

ii) *Mlle Desjardins*

The first contemporary account of *Les Précieuses ridicules* raises an interesting critical question. Mlle Desjardins's *Récit de la farce des Précieuses* probably began to circulate, in manuscript form, in late November 1659. A copy of the manuscript version was preserved by Conrart. According to the author, this version was published without her consent, although no trace of this edition now survives. Another edition followed, in 1660, this time with the author's blessing, and an

unauthorised copy appeared the same year in Antwerp. Such
was the popularity of *Les Précieuses ridicules*!

The importance of the *Récit* stems from the fact that Mlle
Desjardins's account of *Les Précieuses ridicules* is occasionally
at variance with the version subsequently published by Molière.
It begins with what is now scene III, the discussion between
Gorgibus and the servant girl. Then comes that part of scene IV
which mentions the girls' assumed names, and then a scene
which does not feature at all in Molière's text. It shows the girls'
impertinent rejection of the suitors, amid much yawning and
asking the time. Although this sounds very much like the scene
described by La Grange at the beginning of *Les Précieuses
ridicules*, the *Récit* makes it clear that this rejection scene
actually took place on stage: 'peu de temps après la sortie du
vieillard, il vint deux galants offrir leurs services aux
demoiselles' (*14*, p.122). After this comes the rest of scene IV,
but with Magdelon's speech of courtship recounted in verse and
divided into numbered stanzas. Then follow the events of scenes
V-XVII: very little detail is given of the final scenes and Jodelet
is simply described as 'un certain vicomte'.

In addition, the *Récit* slightly increases the role of Gorgibus,
adds slightly to the cosmetics used, fails to prepare the reader for
Mascarille's cleverness and does not make it clear that his visit is
inspired by his master's desire for revenge. It also gets their
names slightly wrong: Magdelon and Cathos decide to call themselves Clymène and Philimène, instead of Polixène and Aminte.
In the manuscript version, Cathos is actually called Margot
throughout.

The manuscript copy also contains two rather broad jokes
which figure neither in the published version of the *Récit* nor in
Molière's text. According to the manuscript, when Mascarille
was announced: 'elles commandèrent qu'on le fît entrer; mais,
en attendant, elles demandèrent une soucoupe inférieure' (*3*,
p.128). But the servant girl found this request for a commode
particularly incomprehensible! Two scenes later, still according
to the manuscript version, Jodelet claimed to have received a
musket ball in the head, which he got rid of by sneezing it out.

Apart from these points, the *Récit* gives an account of the play which corresponds perfectly to Molière's published text, often to the extent of direct quotations. The question it raises is whether or not we can accept it as a faithful account of an early version of *Les Précieuses ridicules*, presumably the one given at the first performance, which was then modified before the play was published.

A potential difficulty concerning Mlle Desjardins's account of the play is that she claims, in her preface, to have written it 'sur le rapport d'autrui' (*14*, p.118), that is, before she had actually seen it for herself. It has been argued that her description therefore refers to a broader form of *Les Précieuses ridicules*, performed as a farce in the provinces before the troupe's return to Paris (*18*, XXIII, pp.1-15). This notion is based largely on the fact that the *Récit* talks of 'La *farce* des Précieuses', whereas Molière's title is *Les Précieuses ridicules, comédie*. On the other hand, the actor La Grange specifically states (*7*, p.998) that *Les Précieuses ridicules* was written in 1659, and the term 'farce' can be easily explained by the presence of the broad humour indicated in the manuscript version. Certain corrections were obviously made between the manuscript copy and the 1660 edition, notably the suppression of the crude jokes and the substitution of Cathos for Margot. On the other hand, the changes were not systematic, as the assumed names remain Clymène and Philimène and the scene between the *précieuses* and their suitors was not suppressed. The presence of the word 'farce' in the title of the published *Récit* may therefore be the result of an oversight. Alternatively, commercial wisdom may have led Mlle Desjardins to retain a title by which the account was already known. She had no obvious reason to want to flatter Molière. Although it has been suggested (*9*, p.31) that she was a friend of his, there is no evidence of any contact between them before Easter 1664, when he began rehearsals of her play *Le Favory*.

It has also been suggested that Mlle Desjardins had indeed not seen the play but that the discrepancies between the *Récit* and Molière's text stem from her desire to please Mme de Morangis, to whom she sent the original description, by developing passages likely to be of interest to her (*8*, p.43). That may well be true of the description of romanesque courtship; and it presumably explains why direct quotations from Molière's prose are to be found in the middle of verse sections of the *Récit*. But the reference to the 'soucoupe inférieure' makes it difficult to accept this hypothesis in its entirety: if Mlle Desjardins were simply intent on making her account agreeable, why include this crude detail in a letter intended for the eyes of a lady whose piety was famous throughout Paris?

Although Tallemant seems to doubt Mlle Desjardins's claim that she had not seen the play (*38*, II, p.901), it is difficult to see why she would say this if it were not true. In any case, the numerous textual similarities between the *Récit* and Molière's published text suggest that she was working on very detailed — and accurate — information. In view of the general accuracy of her account it is difficult to believe that she would have invented the scene with the suitors: it is inconceivable that she would have invented the joke about the 'soucoupe inférieure'. It seems to me more likely that the *Récit* gives an accurate impression of the first performance of *Les Précieuses ridicules*, that is, of the performance given on 18 November 1659. The discrepancies between the *Récit* and Molière's text are not hard to explain. Molière was not originally intending to publish the play and, with Jodelet in the cast, there was doubtless a degree of improvisation about the early performances: it is therefore likely that no two performances were identical.

In addition, Molière may well have chosen to streamline and tone down his play during the two months that elapsed between the first performance and publication. The changes undoubtedly make good sense. It was a wise concession to Parisian taste to suppress the scatalogical humour. And there are clearly advantages in having the rejection scene briefly described by La Grange at the beginning of the play. The entry of the *précieuses* is thus prepared by two vividly contrasting scenes, instead of by Gorgibus alone. The old man's anger is made the more credible if the rejection scene has already taken place. It is also possible that the latter scene, which featured neither of the star comic actors, was just not terribly successful: it may have seemed merely a tame prefiguration of the marvellous Mascarille scenes that were to follow.

It is therefore perfectly feasible that these changes should have been made for sound dramatic and commercial reasons. There is no evidence to support the view that they were imposed on the troupe through the intervention of some mysterious courtier. On the contrary, if the play was originally performed as a fairly unsophisticated farce, then it is even less surprising that Molière was prepared to make way for the indifferent tragedies of Coqueteau and Magnon.

Although the circumstances of the first performances of *Les Précieuses ridicules* were not entirely typical of the plays that were to follow, these changes underline what one might call the 'organic' quality that one sometimes senses elsewhere in Molière's work. Like his Italian masters, Molière was skilled at improvisation and fond of experiment. A certain evolution was therefore possible after the first performance. In at least one case, this process of evolution seems to have continued even after publication (*12*, pp.73-75). This observation supports the view, expressed in Molière's indignant preface, that *Les Précieuses ridicules* was conceived as theatre, not literature. For Molière, if not for Somaize, the distinction was evidently crucial.

iii) *Somaize*

On 12 January 1660, the bookseller Jean Ribou took out a double licence authorising him to print and sell *Les Précieuses ridicules* and *Les Véritables Précieuses*, a comedy by Antoine Baudeau de Somaize. Molière had no reason to publish his play at this time because publication would have cost his troupe the sole performance rights on a work which had clearly not exhausted its popularity in the theatre. Somaize had fraudulently obtained permission to publish Molière's play under cover of obtaining a licence for his own work.

Les Véritables Précieuses is a poor thing, lacking life and originality: clearly modelled on Molière's play, it contains two young *précieuses*, a bogus nobleman and a valet disguised as a poet. Somaize's touch is extremely heavy. His two young girls speak a pretentious jargon so obscure that the author has to add notes to explain his own dialogue: in scene II, for example, Iscarie reprimands Artemise in these terms:

> Vraiment, ma chère, je suis en humeur de pousser le dernier mal[a] contre vous ... le temps a déjà marqué deux pas[b] depuis que je vous attends ... Je crois que vous avez dessein de faire bien des assauts d'appas[c]; je vous trouve dans votre bel aimable.[d] L'invincible n'a pas encore gâté l'économie de votre tête.[e] (*35*, II, pp.11-12)

And Somaize adds, in a marginal note:

> a: De me mettre en colère, b: Deux heures, c: Des conquêtes, d: Belle, e: Le vent n'a point défrisé vos cheveux.

Somaize has fallen into a trap which Molière avoids: this cumbersome dialogue serves to emphasise the lightness and transparency of Molière's own jargon.

Somaize's attempt to publish *Les Précieuses ridicules* was foiled by another bookseller, Guillaume de Luyne, who alerted Molière and had Somaize's licence cancelled; he also obtained another, in Molière's name this time, on 19 January. To prevent a recurrence of Somaize's ploy, Molière had little option but to publish his play: ten days later, it was on sale.

The speed of Molière's response evidently surprised Somaize, whose own play had still not appeared. He reacted by adding a virulent preface to *Les Véritables Précieuses*, in which he repeats, with particular venom, the attacks on Molière already made in the play. His main accusation, one which was to become commonplace among Molière's jealous rivals, is that of plagiarism. As we have seen, there is no hard evidence to support Somaize's allegation that Molière had copied a play by de Pure: it was doubtless just a ploy to deflect attention away from the crudity of his own plagiarism.

Somaize then proceeded to publish four more works in quick succession, all designed to exploit the theme of *préciosité* popularised by Molière's play. After that, Somaize was never heard of again: after eighteen frenzied months of writing and polemic, total silence. His publications are a kind of tribute, a token of the tremendous success of *Les Précieuses ridicules*. Far from doing Molière any harm, his cumbersome pastiches merely emphasise the lightness and brilliance of the original. It is possible that Somaize was encouraged to attack Molière by the actors of the Hôtel de Bourgogne, in response to the joke about their unsubtle style. But, in the absence of libel laws, there was little that Molière could do about Somaize; except, of course, protect his own interests by having *Les Précieuses ridicules* printed, which he might otherwise not have done. Thus, by helping to turn Molière into a published author, Somaize's role in the history of world theatre was unwittingly crucial!

iv) *Molière's preface*

If Somaize's intervention turned Molière into an author, it also turned him into a critic. When *Les Précieuses ridicules* appeared in print, it was accompanied by a fascinating preface which constitutes his first published reflexions on his art. Although presumably written in haste, it is a dignified and witty statement of his position in January 1660: but the implications of what he says in this preface go far beyond the squalid machinations of Somaize.

Such documents are precious because they are rare. We actually know comparatively little about Molière's ideas on theatre. No manuscripts or letters have survived: all we have are his published works. He did once mention the possibility of publishing his thoughts on his profession: 'je ne désespère pas de faire voir un jour que je puis citer Aristote et Horace' (*Avertissement* to *Les Fâcheux*, 1662). But the ironic tone of this passage makes it likely that it is a mocking reference to Pierre Corneille, whose *Trois discours sur le poème dramatique*, bristling with references to Aristotle and Horace, had been published a little over a year earlier. Anyway, the work he mentions never materialised.

All we therefore have, in the way of Molière's reflexions on his profession, are a few short prefaces and the two little polemical plays spawned by the scandal surrounding *L'Ecole des femmes*. This state of affairs is particularly frustrating as the writings we do have suggest that the printed texts give only a pallid outline of what actually went on in his theatres. The wide-ranging preface to *Les Précieuses ridicules* is thus of particular interest.

The starting point is obviously Molière's protest at Somaize's cynical behaviour. It is often forgotten that Molière was not just an artist in his own right. He was also a professional manager running a business which provided over a dozen people with their livelihood: by seventeenth-century standards this was an enormous organisation. The financial cost to the company, if Somaize had succeeded with his scheme, might have been considerable, and so he had to be stopped. Faced with 'la nécessité d'être imprimé ou d'avoir un procès', it clearly made sound commercial sense to settle, however reluctantly, for publication.

Left to himself, he says, he would not have published the play: 'je trouvais que le succès qu'elles [i.e., *Les Précieuses ridicules*] avaient eu dans la représentation était assez beau pour en demeurer là' (ll.14-15). There seems no reason to doubt what he says. It was not customary to publish one-act plays and he had not published the two five-act comedies, theoretically far more suitable for publication, which he had written in the provinces. He never published the unsuccessful *Dom Garcie*, and *Le Cocu imaginaire* was published without his authorisation. He could therefore justifiably claim, in the dedication of *L'Ecole des maris* (1661), that the latter play was the first that he had *chosen* to have printed. He was then almost forty and had been writing for the stage for at least six years.

His lack of real interest in publishing his plays lasted all his life. Eight works remained unpublished at his death, a quarter of his total output.[4] If he chose to publish any at all — always the most successful — it was for sound commercial reasons rather than literary ambition: they represented another source of income and good publicity for the theatre, which was evidently

---

[4] *Dom Garcie, L'Impromptu de Versailles, Dom Juan, Mélicerte, La Pastorale comique, L'Amour médecin, La Comtesse d'Escarbagnas* and *Le Malade imaginaire.*

his main concern.

Hence the mocking tone, in the preface to *Les Précieuses ridicules*, of his reference to literary conventions. If only he had time, he says, he would have written an 'épître dédicatoire bien fleurie', a 'belle et docte préface' and a 'louange en grec'. Such pedantry would of course have been wildly inappropriate in connection with a play like *Les Précieuses ridicules*. The joke is a good one — and characteristic of Molière. Just as his plays show scant respect for the rules of seventeenth-century theatre, so his other published writings tend to poke fun at established literary procedures. In his *Remerciement au Roi* (1663), for example, he manages to thank the king for his generosity while brilliantly satirising the usual turgid ritual of tributes to patrons. In the same way, the preface to *Les Précieuses ridicules* manages to poke fun at the convention of writing prefaces.

Similarly, whereas the prefaces of Corneille's plays are full of learned references to literary theory ancient and modern, that of *Les Précieuses ridicules* simply expresses faith in his audience: 'comme le public est le juge absolu de ces sortes d'ouvrages, il y aurait de l'impertinence à moi de le démentir' (ll.6-8). This simple idea was to be one that Molière repeatedly came back to: few though his critical writings are, he states his fundamental trust in the judgement of the public in almost every one. His characteristic tactic, first defined in the preface to *Les Précieuses ridicules*, is therefore simply to pass over the heads of the theorists and to appeal directly to the spectators. His only criterion is whether a play works in the theatre and is likely to appeal to the public for which it is written.

The artist and the businessman are therefore sometimes hard to separate. If these values sound modest, even faintly vulgar, it must be admitted that they were to some extent thrust upon Molière by commercial reality: on the other hand, they enabled him to prise French comedy free from conventional romanticism through his willingness constantly to experiment with new comic forms. *Les Précieuses ridicules* is the first of these experiments and its preface records his faintly surprised pleasure at the way it has been received: 'quand j'aurais eu la plus mauvaise opinion du monde de mes *Précieuses ridicules* avant leur représentation, je dois croire maintenant qu'elles valent quelque chose' (ll.8-10).

But perhaps the most revealing aspect of this preface is the reason Molière gives for not wanting to publish the play: 'comme une grande partie des grâces qu'on y a trouvées dépendent de l'action et du ton de voix, il m'importait qu'on ne les dépouillât pas de ces ornements (ll.11-13). This is the statement of a showman, not of a writer. And it certainly transcends the question of whether a humble *petit divertissement* ought to be published. Five years later he developed the same idea in relation to a comedy commissioned by the king: 'On sait bien que les comédies ne sont faites que pour être jouées et je ne conseille de lire celle-ci qu'aux personnes qui ont des yeux pour découvrir, dans la lecture, tout le jeu du théâtre' (*L'Amour médecin*, 'Au lecteur'). This attitude, the antithesis of Somaize's self-publicising cynicism, reflects the deepest possible respect for the nature of theatre: that is, the all-round theatrical impact, in comedy at least, as distinct from the more literary appeal of a poet like Corneille. Even the hostile critic Donneau de Visé, in the midst of his attack on *L'Ecole des femmes*, had to admit the care and thought that went into *every* aspect of Molière's productions (*26*, I, p.177). They were invariably highly visual, making their impact through finely judged spectacle and movement, as well as words: Mascarille's ludicrous wig and mincing gait are as important as his jargon. This is why, in order properly to understand *Les Précieuses ridicules*, we owe it to Molière to consider relevant details of casting and costume, as well as the text of the play.

The final point raised by the preface concerns the kind of impact the play was seeking to make. Molière speaks of his wish to 'justifier mes intentions' (l.43), which suggests the latter were being discussed and possibly criticised. The topicality of the subject was something new on the comic stage and there was clearly a danger of being misunderstood. Molière is therefore concerned to define the nature of the intended satire: 'les véritables précieuses auraient tort de se piquer lorsqu'on joue les ridicules qui les imitent mal' (ll.53-54). Again, this is the first statement of an argument that was to become familiar. Because of the controversial subjects of his plays and the sharpness of his

Conclusion

It has been suggested that *Les Précieuses ridicules* destroyed *préciosité*. Writing 30 years after the first performance, Charles Perrault claimed that the play's impact was such that 'toute la nation des précieuses s'éteignit en moins de quinze jours' (*29*, I, p.80). Most of the evidence, however, suggests that the blow it struck was not mortal. Molière himself returns to the subject of *préciosité* in *La Critique de l'Ecole des femmes* (1663) and in *Les Femmes savantes* (1672). Anthologies written in the style appreciated by the *précieuses* continued to be published until the end of the century: the *Recueil La Suze-Pellisson* alone had 16 editions between 1663 and 1698. Moreover, the portraits of Acis and Cydias in La Bruyère's *Caractères* (1668), as well as Boursault's comedy *Les Mots à la mode* (1694) and the continuing popularity of *Les Précieuses ridicules* itself all suggest that affected manners and speech were still recognisable features of French society three decades after the first performance of Molière's play.

This is not particularly surprising: if affectation tends to be a prominent feature of heavily stratified societies, it is also a constant human foible which belongs to no particular age. A single play, however brilliant, could never wipe it out. If *Les Précieuses ridicules* had really destroyed the pretentiousness it satirises, it would now be of merely historical interest. This is clearly not the case. If the term *précieux* itself fell from fashion in the early 1660s, the pretentiousness behind it lived on: Molière's achievement is not to have reformed society but to have demonstrated that affectation could be amusingly parodied in the theatre.

The influence of *Les Précieuses ridicules* is therefore theatrical rather than sociological. It was an experimental play and the success of the experiment is reflected in much of Molière's later work. For example, the blend of farce and social satire, first tried in *Les Précieuses ridicules*, became a characteristic feature of his plays: even *Le Misanthrope* contains moments of farce. Like Mascarille, many of Molière's greatest characters imagine themselves to be something they are not: the comic rigidity of characters like Harpagon and Monsieur Jourdain is faintly reminiscent of the *mask* convention. *Le Médecin malgré lui* has in common with *Les Précieuses ridicules* the theme of revenge and the curious detail of an impostor who clings to his role even after he has been unmasked. And jargon of various kinds provides an important source of comedy in plays as varied as *La Critique de l'Ecole des femmes*, *Tartuffe* and *Le Malade imaginaire*. If it is unlikely that Molière took all these ideas directly from *Les Précieuses ridicules*, it is interesting to note the presence in his first Parisian work of so many important features of his later plays.

Although Mascarille himself does not appear in any subsequent play by Molière, the legacy of his role in *Les Précieuses ridicules* is considerable. His fame was such that he makes a brief reappearance in Chevalier's *Les Amours de Calotin* (1663) and there are references to him in Boursault's *Le Médecin volant* (1664) and Le Noble's *Les Barons fléchois* (1665). In Molière's theatre, foolish *marquis* figure prominently in several later plays, culminating in the outrageous fops of *Le Misanthrope*: one of the anti-Molière plays spawned by the controversy over *L'Ecole des femmes* was actually entitled *La Vengeance des marquis*. The animosity of the Hôtel de Bourgogne during this quarrel had been fuelled by Mascarille's comment on its actors' declamatory style. Molière's response to their attacks was *L'Impromptu de Versailles*, in which he develops Mascarille's comparison of the two troupes into a brilliant parody of his rivals' technique and an ironic defence of his own more naturalistic style.

The play which owes most to *Les Précieuses ridicules* is of course *Les Femmes savantes*. Molière frequently looked for inspiration to his own earlier works. The passages on jealousy in *Dom Garcie de Navarre* recur in *Le Misanthrope*; and *Le Médecin volant* was almost certainly combined with the anonymous farce *Le Fagotier* to produce *Le Médecin par force*, which subsequently became *Le Médecin malgré lui*. But the most elaborate example of this technique is the systematic way in which *Les Précieuses ridicules* was developed, 13 years later, into the five-act comedy *Les Femmes savantes*. The emphasis changes from literary snobbery to pedantry in general and the relationships become far more complex. But all the characters in the farce have their counterparts in the later play. The two 'pecques provinciales' become three 'femmes savantes'; Bélise, like Magdelon, is unable to distinguish between reality and romantic fiction; Armande, like Cathos, wants to be wooed while claiming to reject physical love; and Philaminte, the most pretentious of the three, sacks the servant for not speaking in the manner of the gentry. The prosaic and irascible Chrysale owes much to Gorgibus; La Grange and Du Croisy, down to earth aristocrats, are transformed into Clitandre and Henriette, perhaps the most likeable pair of lovers in Molière's theatre; and Mascarille and Jodelet become the cynical and vulgar poets Trissotin and Vadius. In *Les Femmes savantes*, as in *Les Précieuses ridicules*, mediocre poetry is submitted to a grotesquely flattering analysis; the contest to show the biggest scar has its equivalent in the quarrel over the poems; in both plays, a plan to create a learned society is vaguely discussed; and Chrysale, like Gorgibus, complains of the 'brimborions' with which these irksome women are filling his house.

If *Les Précieuses ridicules* influenced aspects of Molière's later plays, it also had an effect on those of his contemporaries. One immediate result of the play's success was a general resurgence of farce on the Parisian stage. The theatrical form which had been virtually killed off by the influence of the *précieuses* was thus brought back into fashion by a play which makes fun of them. This sudden vogue was remarkable. In 1660 alone there were new farces by Montfleury, Villiers and Chevalier, as well as Molière's own *Sganarelle*; at the end of the same year, Dorimond's troupe treated the Parisian public to some of the farces which had long been popular in Lyons. And the fashion was to last. Antoine Adam has calculated that, of 37 new comedies performed between 1663 and 1667, 24 consisted of one act only (*11*, p.412). In the dedication to *Les Barons fléchois* (published in 1667), the author justifies his abandonment of the five-act form on the grounds that he considers the work a farce, now a popular kind of play (*21*, III, p.675). In his *Registre*, La Grange mentions a dozen or so farces performed by Molière's troupe, from 1660 onwards, which never found their way into print. Some were doubtless by Molière himself. Of his extant works, 8 are 'pure' farces, a quarter of his total output.

Another feature of French comedy in the 1660s which *Les Précieuses ridicules* helped on its way was comedy of manners. Molière himself soon became famous for his carefully observed *marquis*, bigots, social climbers and doctors. But his contemporaries had also begun to exploit this rich vein: in the comedies of this period by Chevalier, Jean de la Forge, Donneau de Visé, Hauteroche and Poisson, we find subjects ranging from gambling to gastronomy, foolish country squires to the latest in public transport. It would be unrealistic to claim that *Les Précieuses ridicules* alone was responsible for this fashion; but we have noted the originality of Molière's play in this respect and its success undoubtedly speeded up the development of this kind of comedy.

Its fame spread to England, where several major authors paid Molière the compliment of imitating his work.[5] It entered the repertoire of the Comédie-Française on the latter's creation in 1680 and was performed there 76 times before the end of the century. In the 18th century, it was particularly popular at court: under Louis XV and Louis XVI it was, after *La Comtesse d'Escarbagnas*, the Molière play most frequently performed at Versailles. It was also the last play to be performed at Versailles before the Revolution. In all, up to 31 December 1983, *Les Précieuses ridicules* had been performed 1268 times at the Comédie-Française: in terms of performances of all Molière's plays, this figure puts it in 11th place, just behind *Le Bourgeois gentilhomme*.

Although basically a farce written in a moment of crisis and intended for a particular group of actors, *Les Précieuses ridicules* is also an exquisitely crafted blend of elements from a

[5] Richard Flecknoe's *The Damoiselles à la Mode* (1667), Mrs Aphra Benn's *The False Count* (1682) and Thomas Shadwell's *Bury Fair* (1689).

highly original variety of sources: it is an exuberant mixture of visual gags, verbal wit, social satire and the first glimmerings of character comedy, which effectively pushed back the boundaries of farce. It represents a decisive step forward in the development of Molière's dramatic technique and anticipates many features of the full-length comedies that were to follow. Unpretentious though it is, it has been called the first comic masterpiece in the French language since the *Farce de Maître Pathelin* (5, p.48). If the general public of today knows anything of the *précieuses*, it is thanks to the enduring freshness of Molière's little play.

Bibliography

Unless stated otherwise, the works below were published in Paris.

EDITIONS OF LES PRÉCIEUSES RIDICULES MENTIONED

1. Luyne, G. de. January, 1660.
2. La Grange & Vivot. *Les Œuvres de M. de Molière*, Thierry, Barbin & Trabouillet, 1682, 8 vols, I, pp.219-63.
3. Despois, Eugène & Mesnard, Paul. *Molière, Œuvres*, Grands Ecrivains de France, Hachette, 1873-1900, 13 vols, II, pp.3-134.
4. Livet, Ch.-L. Dupont, 1884.
5. Ledésert, R.P.L. London, Harrap, 1948.
6. Balcou, Jean. Nouveaux Classiques Larousse, 1970.
7. Couton, Georges. *Molière, Œuvres complètes*, Bibliothèque de la Pléiade, Gallimard, 1971, 2 vols, I, pp.247-87.
8. Cuénin, Micheline. Droz, 1973.
9. Angué, Fernand. Univers des Lettres, Bordas, 1962.

OTHER WORKS CONSULTED

10. Adam, Antoine. 'La genèse des *Précieuses ridicules*', *Revue d'histoire de la philosophie et d'histoire générale de la civilisation*, Jan.-March 1939, pp.14-46.
11. ——. *Histoire de la littérature française au XVIIe siècle*, Domat, 1953, 5 vols, vol.III.
12. Bray, René. *Molière, homme de théâtre*, Mercure de France, 1954.
13. Brunetière, Ferdinand. *Etudes critiques sur l'histoire de la littérature classique française*, Hachette, 1904, 8 vols.
14. Desjardins, Marie-Catherine. *Récit de la farce des Précieuses* (Barbin, 1660), reprinted in Despois, II, pp.118-34.
15. Faure. *La Fine Galanterie du temps*, Ribou, 1661.
16. Fukui, Y. *Raffinement précieux dans la poésie française du XVIIe siècle*, Nizet, 1964.
17. Howarth, W.D. *Molière, a Playwright and his Audience*, Cambridge University Press, 1982.
18. Lacroix, Paul. *Collection moliéresque*, Paris & Geneva, Jouaust, 1867-90, 37 vols, reprinted Geneva, Slatkine, 1968-69.
19. La Fontaine, Jean. *Clymène* (Barbin, 1671) in *La Fontaine, Œuvres diverses*, Bibliothèque de la Pléiade, Gallimard, 1958, pp.20-46.
20. La Grange, Charles Varlet de. *Registre 1659-1685*, facsimile edition (ed. B.E. Young & G.P. Young), Droz, 1947, 2 vols.

21. Lancaster, H. Carrington. *A History of French Dramatic Literature in the Seventeenth Century*, Baltimore, Johns Hopkins Press, 1929-42, 10 vols.

22. Lanson, Gustave. 'Molière et la farce', *Revue de Paris*, May 1901, pp.129-53.

23. Larroumet, Gustave. 'Un historien de la société précieuse du XVIIe siècle, Baudeau de Somaize', *Revue des Deux Mondes*, 112, July 1892, pp.124-55.

24. Lathuillère, Roger. *La Préciosité*, Droz, 1966.

25. Livet, Ch.-L. *Lexique de la langue de Molière*, Imprimerie Nationale, 1895-97, 3 vols.

26. Michaut, Gustave. *Les Débuts de Molière à Paris*, Hachette, 1923.

27. Mongrédien, Georges. *Recueil des textes et des documents du XVIIe siècle relatifs à Molière*, C.N.R.S., 1965, 2 vols.

28. Montpensier, Anne-Marie-Louise, duchesse de. *Divers portraits*, Caen, 1659.

29. Perrault, Charles. *Les Hommes illustres qui ont paru en France pendant ce siècle*, Dezallier, 1696.

30. Pure, Michel, abbé de. *La Prétieuse ou le Mystère des ruelles* (De Luyne, 1656-58), reprinted by E. Magne, Droz, 1938-39, 2 vols.

31. Scarron, Paul. *Œuvres*, Amsterdam, 1752, 7 vols.

32. ——. *Le Roman comique* (Quinet & De Luyne, 1651-57), reprinted by E. Magne, Garnier, 1955.

33. Scudéry, Madeleine de. *Artamène ou le grand Cyrus* (Courbé, 1649-53, 10 vols), reprinted Geneva, Slatkine, 1972.

34. Sévigné, Renaud, Chevalier de. *Correspondance du chevalier de Sévigné et de Christine de France*, ed. Lemoine & Saulnier, Société de l'Histoire de France, 1911.

35. Somaize, Antoine Baudeau de. *Dictionnaire des Précieuses, etc.*, ed. C.L. Livet, Jannet, 1856, 2 vols.

36. Sorel, Charles. *Les Lois de la galanterie*, Sercy, 1658 (augmented edn).

37. ——. *De la connaissance des bons livres* (Pralard, 1671), reprinted by Lucia Moretti Cenerini, Rome, Bulzoni, 1974.

38. Tallemant des Réaux, Gédéon. *Historiettes* (first published by Monmerqué, 1834-35, 6 vols), reprinted by A. Adam, Bibliothèque de la Pléiade, Gallimard, 1960-61, 2 vols.

CRITICAL GUIDES TO FRENCH TEXTS

edited by

Roger Little, Wolfgang van Emden, David Williams